# International Primary
# SCIENCE 6

## Student's Book

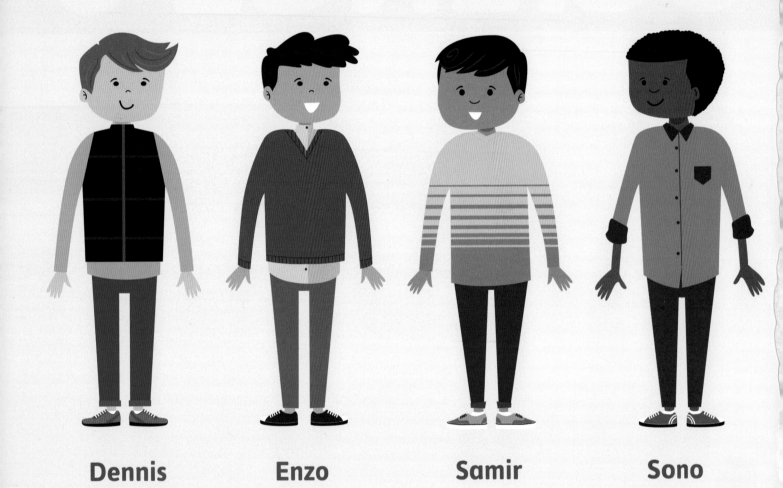

**Dennis**     **Enzo**     **Samir**     **Sono**

Emma　　　Luna　　　Maya　　　Yin

# Contents

Biology     Chemistry     Physics

# 1 🧬 Body Systems

## 1.1 What are the major body organs?

**Keywords**
abdomen   body system   brain   chest   heart
identify   intestines   kidney   lung   major   organ
properly   stomach

**Let's think**

Inside the human body there are different parts. Each of them has a job to do and they work together to keep us alive and healthy.

**A**

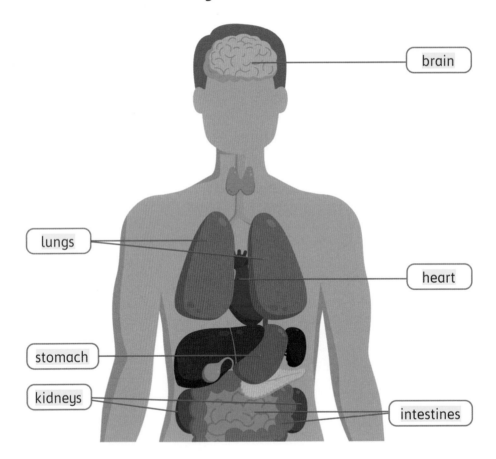

- brain
- lungs
- heart
- stomach
- kidneys
- intestines

The different parts of our bodies are the organs. Some organs work together to form a body system. Each body system does a specific function. Body systems also work together. All major organs have very important functions in the human body. We cannot stay alive if a major organ cannot do its function properly.

Identify the position of each major organ in the human body.

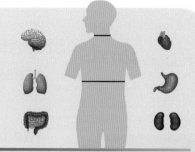

##  Let's explore!

- Where are the major organs inside our body?
- Put the major organs in their positions inside the human body.
- Present your model to the class.

 Which organs are in the head, which are in the chest and which are in the abdomen?

**B**

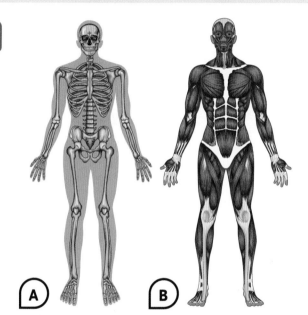

Bones and muscles are also organs that work together to form body systems.

How do the bones and the muscles work together?

 How are your heart and brain protected?

Science in action

Starfish are animals with no brain. Can humans live without a brain?

- **The organs are parts of our bodies that work together to form body systems.**
- **The major organs are the heart, the brain, the lungs, the stomach, the intestines and the kidneys.**

# 1.2 How does the nervous system work?

**Keywords** brainstem carry cerebellum cerebrum control message nerve nervous system spinal cord

**Let's think**

The brain is the major organ of the **nervous system**. The nervous system helps different parts of the body to work together, and **controls** all other body systems.

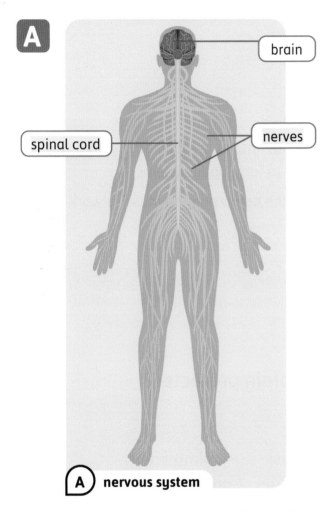

**A** nervous system

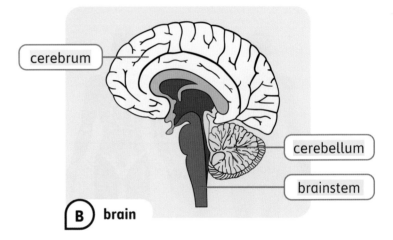

**B** brain

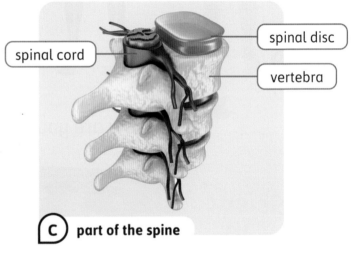

**C** part of the spine

The nervous system is made up of the brain, the spinal cord and all the nerves in the body.

The brain is a soft organ inside the skull. It controls our thoughts and emotions, our speech and movement, and the function of many organs in the body. The brain has three main parts, the cerebrum, the cerebellum and the brainstem. Each part has its own functions.

The brainstem connects the brain to the spinal cord.

The spinal cord contains nerves that connect the different organs and body parts to the brain.

1. What parts of the body protect the brain and the spinal cord?

2. Why is it important that the brain and the spinal cord are protected?

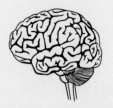

 **Let's explore!**

- Search for information about what the different parts of the brain control.
- Look in books or on the Internet.
- Present your findings to the class.

**(?)** What do the cerebrum, the cerebellum and the brainstem control?

**B**

The nervous system allows us to sense different things. One kind of nerve connects the sense organs of the body to the brain through the spinal cord. These nerves carry messages from in and around the body to the brain and the brain sends, through a different kind of nerve, messages to the muscles to make us respond. These messages are carried quickly.

Why is it important for the messages between the body and the brain to be carried quickly?

*Science in action*

After a spinal cord injury it often happens that messages cannot pass through the spinal cord to and from the brain. Why do people with such an injury often use a wheelchair?

- **The brain, the spinal cord and the nerves are the parts of the nervous system.**
- **The brain has three main parts, the cerebrum, the cerebellum and the brainstem.**
- **The brain controls different functions of our body by sending and receiving messages through the spinal cord and the nerves.**

# 1.3 How does the circulatory system work?

**Keywords**

artery   be poor in   be rich in   beat   blood
blood vessel   circulation   circulatory system
heartbeat   pulse   pump   rate   remove   trend   vein

**Let's think**

The heart is the major organ of the **circulatory system**. The heart moves the **blood** in the circulatory system all around the body.

**A**

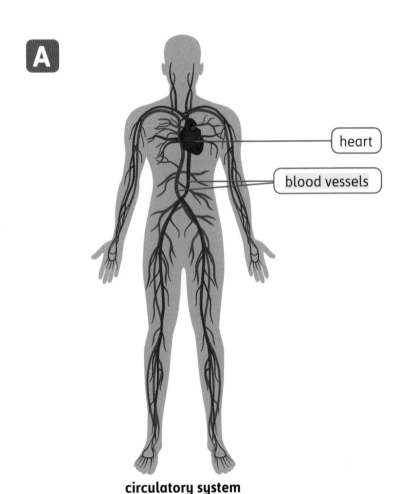

heart

blood vessels

circulatory system

The circulatory system is made up of the heart, the blood vessels and the blood.

The heart is protected by the ribcage. The heart is a muscle that you cannot control. It contracts to pump blood through the body. The movement of the blood around the body is called circulation.

The blood moves around the body in blood vessels, like arteries that carry blood from the heart to the body and veins that carry blood from the body to the heart. The blood carries substances from food and oxygen from the air to different parts of the body, and removes waste products from the different parts of the body.

Why is it important to have blood vessels around the body?

**B**

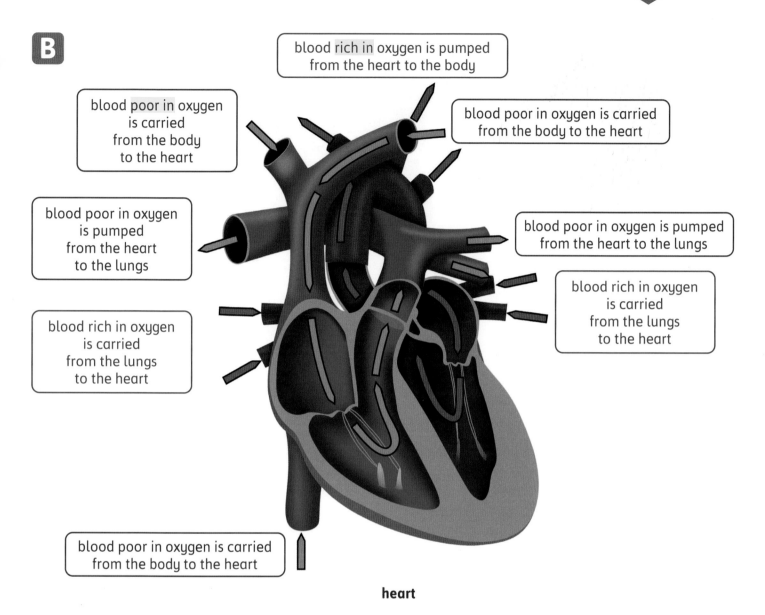

blood rich in oxygen is pumped from the heart to the body

blood poor in oxygen is carried from the body to the heart

blood poor in oxygen is carried from the body to the heart

blood poor in oxygen is pumped from the heart to the lungs

blood poor in oxygen is pumped from the heart to the lungs

blood rich in oxygen is carried from the lungs to the heart

blood rich in oxygen is carried from the lungs to the heart

blood poor in oxygen is carried from the body to the heart

**heart**

The heart contracts and relaxes all the time, even when we sleep. The left side of the heart, red in colour in the picture, receives blood rich in oxygen from the lungs, and pumps it around the body. Blood poor in oxygen returns to the right side of the heart, blue in colour in the picture, and is pumped to the lungs.

The heart pumps blood rich in oxygen to the body. There, the blood gives out oxygen, and gets carbon dioxide produced by the body.

Then, the blood poor in oxygen returns to the heart, and the heart pumps the blood to the lungs. In the lungs, blood gives out carbon dioxide and gets new oxygen. Then, the blood rich in oxygen goes to the heart, and the cycle is repeated. Through breathing, the lungs insert oxygen into the body and remove carbon dioxide from the body.

Why does the blood have to pass through the lungs?

Each time our heart contracts there is a heartbeat. With each heartbeat, blood is pumped into our arteries, causing them to stretch. The movement of the arteries as they stretch and come back to their natural size is a pulse.

The heart of a healthy adult beats about sixty to eighty times in a minute. The rate of the heartbeat changes with age and exercise.

1. How does the heart of a child beat compared to the heart of an adult?

2. Do you think our heart beats faster when we sit or when we exercise?

## 👓 Let's explore!

- Investigate how exercise affects your pulse rate.
- Make a prediction.
- Plan a fair test.
- Do the test and record your results.
- Can you identify a trend in your results?
- Discuss and draw a conclusion.

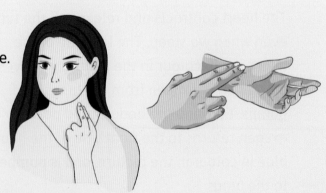

(?) Why does your pulse rate change when you exercise?

Does our heart stop beating when we sleep? Explain your answer.

**D**

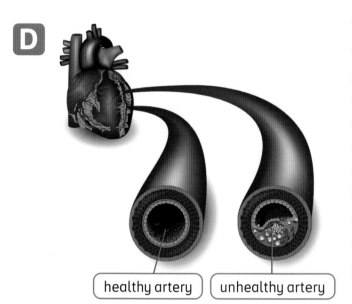

healthy artery | unhealthy artery

The heart is an organ that also needs substances from food, oxygen from the air, and to remove waste products. Exercising makes the muscles of your body stronger, and the muscle of your heart more able to pump blood around the body. A balanced diet is important for the heart. There are some kinds of arteries, that provide the heart with blood rich in oxygen. An unhealthy diet makes these arteries narrower and less elastic. If one of these arteries gets blocked, the person may have a heart attack.

How is a heart attack caused?

*Science in action*

A horse has about 36 heartbeats per minute, a goat has about 70 heartbeats per minute, while a cat has about 195 heartbeats per minute. Do you see a pattern between the size of the animals and their pulse rate? Explain your answer.

- **The circulatory system is made up of the heart, the blood vessels and the blood.**
- **The heart is a muscle that pumps the blood around the body.**
- **The pulse rate increases with exercise.**
- **Exercise and a healthy diet help the circulatory system work well.**

# 1.4 How does the respiratory system work?

Keywords

air sac   breath   diaphragm   respiration
respiratory system   trachea

**Let's think**

The lungs are the major organs of the **respiratory system**. For every **breath** we take, we move air into and out of our lungs.

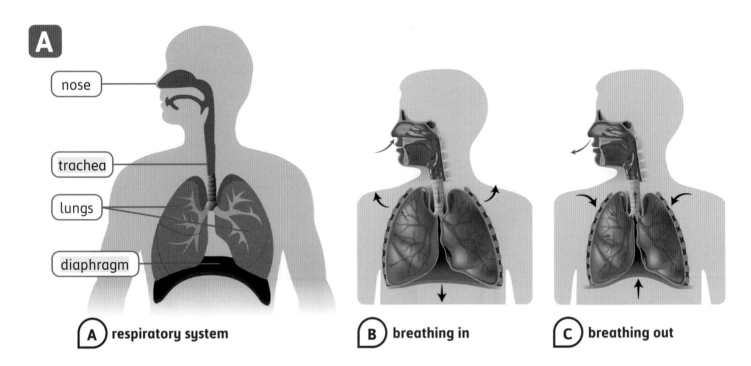

A

nose

trachea

lungs

diaphragm

(A) respiratory system     (B) breathing in     (C) breathing out

The respiratory system is made up of the nose, the trachea and the lungs. The lungs are in the chest, protected by the ribcage. The diaphragm is a muscle we use in breathing.

When we breathe in, the diaphragm contracts and moves down, causing the space in the chest to get bigger, and air to move inside the lungs.

When we breathe out, the diaphragm relaxes and moves up, causing the space in the chest to get smaller again, and air to move out of the lungs.

Why do you think it is important to breathe?

 The air around us is a mixture of gases. Most of the air is made up of nitrogen. Air is also made up of oxygen, carbon dioxide and other gases.

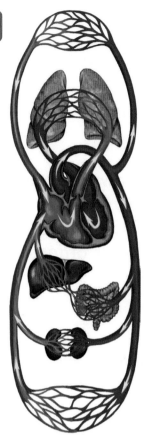

When we breathe in, air passes from the nose or the mouth through the trachea to the lungs. The lungs are made up of little air sacs that have many blood vessels around them.

Oxygen in the air moves from the air sacs into the blood. The blood vessels carry the blood rich in oxygen to the heart, and the heart pumps the blood around the body.

Oxygen is used in the different parts of the body for respiration. During respiration, the energy that is stored in food is released, and carbon dioxide and water are produced. Carbon dioxide is a waste product that has to be removed from the body. So, the blood gives out oxygen, and gets carbon dioxide produced by the body.

The blood vessels bring the blood poor in oxygen, but with more carbon dioxide than before, back to the heart, and the heart pumps it into the lungs. Carbon dioxide in the blood is moved to the air sacs, and then it is removed from the body with the air we breathe out. The cycle is repeated.

How do the respiratory system and the circulatory system work together so that respiration can take place in the different parts of the body?

##  Let's explore!

- Investigate how exercise affects your breathing rate.
- Make a prediction.
- Plan a fair test.
- Do the test and record your results.
- Can you identify a trend in your results?
- Discuss and draw a conclusion.

(?) Why do we breathe faster when we exercise?

- **The nose, the trachea and the lungs are parts of the respiratory system.**
- **The respiratory system brings oxygen inside the body and removes carbon dioxide from the body.**
- **During respiration, the body uses oxygen and produces carbon dioxide.**
- **The breathing rate increases with exercise.**

# 1.5 How does the digestive system work?

Keywords

break down     digest     digestion     digestive juice
digestive system     large intestine     liver
oesophagus     saliva     small intestine

**Let's think**

We need food to survive. Food helps us grow and provides us with energy. Food has to be broken down by the process of digestion so that it can be used by the body. The stomach and the intestines are the major organs of the digestive system.

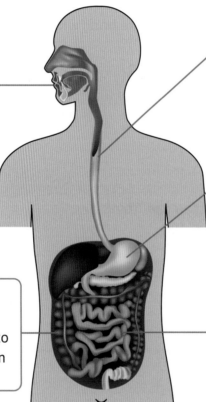

**A**

**1. Mouth**

We chew the food with the teeth, breaking it down into smaller pieces, while it is mixed with saliva. Substances in the saliva start digesting the food.

**2. Oesophagus**

The chewed food is swallowed, and passes through the oesophagus to the stomach.

**3. Stomach**

The stomach produces digestive juices that mix with the food breaking it down further and turning it into a liquid mixture. This liquid food passes slowly into the small intestine.

**5. Large intestine**

Food that hasn't been or can't be digested passes into the large intestine, and then passes out of the body.

**4. Small intestine**

Liquid food mixes with more digestive juices inside the small intestine, and nutrients from the food are broken down further into simpler substances. These substances are absorbed by the small intestine, and enter the blood.

digestive system

The digestive system is made up of the mouth, the oesophagus, the stomach, the small intestine and the large intestine. The digestive system breaks down the food into simpler substances that move into the blood, and are carried around the body.

1. Where does digestion start and where does it end?

2. How are substances from the digested food carried around the body?

**B**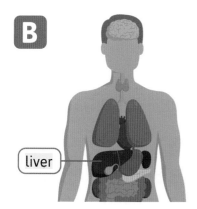

liver

The liver is a very important organ that we cannot live without. It has many different functions. The liver produces a digestive juice, which is released into the small intestine. This digestive juice helps the body absorb fats into the blood. The liver also stores substances from food that provide the body with energy when needed. Another important function of the liver is that it cleans the body's natural waste products and other harmful substances from the blood. These substances are excreted out of the liver, and finally leave the body through the intestines.

Which body systems does the liver help?

## 👀 Let's explore!

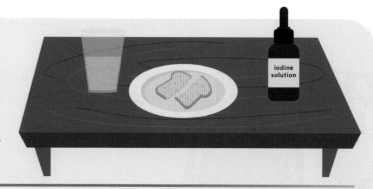

iodine solution

- Investigate if saliva starts digesting food.
- Make a prediction.
- Do the test and record your observations.
- Discuss and draw a conclusion.

 Does digestion happen in the mouth?

Science in action

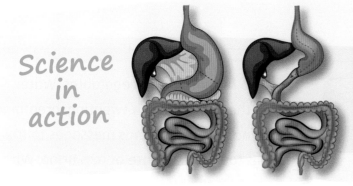

Some stomach problems can only be treated by removing part or all of the stomach. Why do people with part or all of their stomach removed have to eat small meals and chew their food a lot before swallowing it?

- **The mouth, the oesophagus, the stomach, the small intestine and the large intestine are the parts of the digestive system.**
- **The digestive system breaks down food into forms that are carried around the body in the blood, through the circulatory system.**
- **The liver is an important organ in the human body.**

# 1.6 What is the function of the kidneys in the excretory system?

Keywords dialysis excretion excretory system filter urea urine

**Let's think**

The human body produces waste products during different functions. The waste products have to be removed from the body because they will become harmful. The process of removing waste products from the body is called **excretion**.

**A**

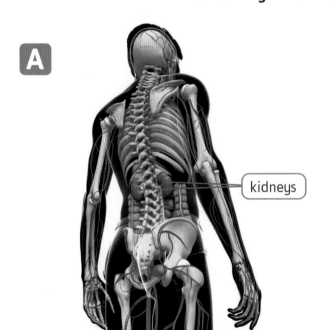

kidneys

The **excretory system** is made up of organs that excrete waste products from the body. The kidneys are a pair of organs that are part of the excretory system. The kidneys are in the back of the body, below the ribcage, on both sides of the spine. The kidneys **filter** blood to remove waste products from it, like salts and **urea**. The waste products are dissolved in water and excreted from the body as **urine**.

Do you know other organs that excrete waste products from your body?

**B**

Another function of the kidneys is to control the amount of water in the blood. Water is very important for the body. We get water when we drink water or other liquids, and also from fruit and vegetables. Water leaves the body through sweating, breathing and urine. The brain sends messages to the kidneys to produce more or less urine. When the water in the blood decreases, e.g. if you sweat a lot, the brain sends a message to the kidneys to make less urine. When there is too much water in the blood, the brain sends a message to the kidneys to make more urine.

Which body systems work together to control the amount of water in the blood?

 **Let's explore!**

- Search for information about what we can do to keep our kidneys healthy.
- Look in books or on the Internet.
- Present your findings to the class.

 What can we do to keep our kidneys healthy?

*Science in action*

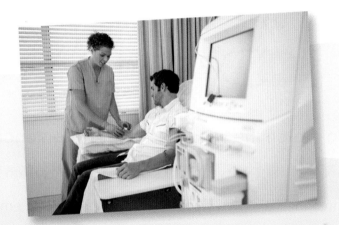

People can live with one kidney, but they cannot live if both kidneys don't work properly. These people need to have waste products removed from their blood, a process called dialysis. Why do people with unhealthy kidneys need dialysis?

- **The kidneys are part of the excretory system.**
- **The kidneys are in the back of the body, below the ribcage, on both sides of the spine.**
- **The kidneys filter the blood to remove waste products from it.**
- **The kidneys control the amount of water in the blood.**

# Review

Go to the **Unit maps** section at the back of the book.

1. In which body system does each organ or pair of organs belong? Match. Write **1-5** in the boxes.

> **1.** nervous system   **2.** circulatory system   **3.** respiratory system
> **4.** digestive system   **5.** excretory system

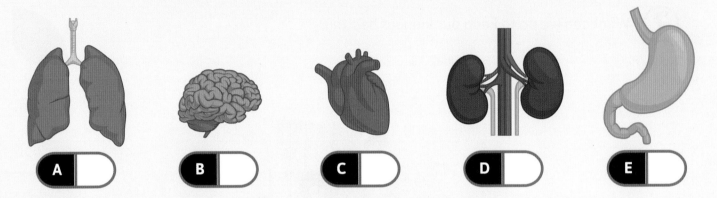

A   B   C   D   E

2. Draw lines to match the two parts of each sentence.

**1.** The liver                    breaks down nutrients from food.

**2.** The small intestine          controls our thoughts and emotions, our speech and movement.

**3.** The trachea                  carry blood to different parts of the body.

**4.** The brain                    cleans the blood of the body's natural waste products.

**5.** The arteries                 control the amount of water in the blood.

**6.** The kidneys                  transports air to and from the lungs.

3. Read the sentences. Write **Yes** or **No**.

**1.** When we lose a lot of water through sweating, the kidneys make more urine. _____

**2.** The lungs are protected by the skull. _____

**3.** The heart contracts and relaxes all the time, even when we sleep. _____

**4.** Carbon dioxide is excreted from our body when we breathe out. _____

**5.** The liver produces a digestive juice that helps the body absorb fat into the blood. _____

**6.** The kidneys are in the front of the body. _____

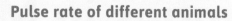

**4.** Look at the bar chart. Then answer the questions.

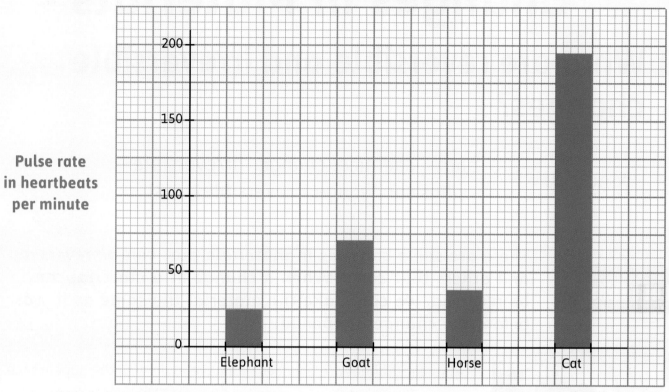

**Pulse rate of different animals**

Pulse rate in heartbeats per minute

Animals

**1.** Which animal has the slowest pulse rate?

_____

_____

**2.** Which animal has the fastest pulse rate?

_____

_____

**3.** Which animal's heart beats slowest and which beats fastest? How can you tell?

_____

_____

_____

_____

**4.** What does the heart do when it beats faster?

_____

_____

_____

# 2  Reversible and Irreversible Changes in Materials

## 2.1 What are reversible and irreversible changes?

**Keywords**   burn   chemical change   irreversible   physical change   reversible   rust

**Let's think**

There are some changes in materials that can be reversed, and others that can't. When a change in a material can be reversed, we can make the material the same as it was before the change happened.

**A**

A

B

Physical changes are changes that have to do with the appearance, shape, form or state of a material. Chemical changes include the production of a new substance.

1. Which change in pictures A and B is a physical change and which is a chemical change?

2. Which change can be reversed and which can't?

3. For the change that can be reversed, propose a process through which we can make the material the same as it was.

### 👀 Let's explore!

- Is burning a candle a change that can be reversed?
- Record your prediction.
- What forms above the candle flame while it is burning?
- Record your observations.
- Discuss and draw a conclusion.

**(?)** Is burning a candle a reversible change or an irreversible change?

**B**

A

B

There are changes that can be reversed, and after which we can make the material the same as it was before the change happened. These changes are reversible. Most physical changes are reversible changes. There are also other changes that can't be reversed, and after which we cannot make the material the same as it was. These changes are irreversible. Most chemical changes in which a new substance forms from other substances

that join together, are irreversible.

When iron or steel nails come into contact with oxygen from the air or water, they rust. When objects made of iron or steel rust, a red-brown substance forms on their surface, because an amount of the material changes into rust.

Are melting and rusting reversible or irreversible changes? Explain your answer.

*Science in action*

Plastic is one among several materials that can be recycled and reused. When plastic objects, like bottles or plastic bags, are recycled, they are at first melted at very high temperatures, and then, their shape is changed to make other plastic objects, like toys, furniture, etc. Why do the processes that take place in recycling need to be reversible?

- **Changes in materials can be reversible or irreversible.**
- **Most physical changes are reversible and most chemical changes are irreversible.**

# 2.2 How can different solids be mixed and separated?

Keywords  *mix  mixture  separate  sieve*

**Let's think**

When we mix solid materials, mixtures in the solid state form. There are several ways in which we can separate solid mixtures and get each solid material back.

**A**

How can you collect only the black beans from the mixture?

## Let's explore!

- Investigate how you can separate different solid mixtures.
- What are the components of the mixtures that you have?
- Do the test and record your observations.
- Are there any mixtures that you can't separate?
- Discuss and draw a conclusion.

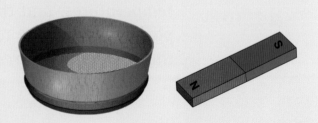

**?** What are some ways of separating solid mixtures?

!  Not all metals are attracted by magnets.

**B**

A

B

C

When solid materials are mixed and no chemical change happens, a mixture is formed. Since no chemical change happens, the materials mixed are not joined together to form a new substance, and this means that we can separate each solid material out.

We can separate solid mixtures by hand, by sieving, or by using a magnet. When the pieces of a solid component are large in size, we can usually collect them from a mixture with our hands. Sieves can be used to separate solid components of a mixture that have different sizes. Sieves can have holes that are smaller or bigger in size, and they hold inside them those solids which are too big to pass through the holes. Magnets can also be used to separate solids, because they attract only magnetic materials.

How can you separate the solid components of each mixture?

*Science in action*

Soil is a mixture of different components. Gardeners sometimes need to remove the rocks and the lumps of soil from the soil before they grow plants in it. How do they separate the rocks and lumps of soil from the soil?

- **Solid mixtures form when we mix solid materials and no chemical change happens.**
- **The materials in a mixture are not joined together, so we can separate them and get them back.**
- **We can separate solid mixtures by hand, by sieving, and by using a magnet.**

# 2.3 What happens when we mix solids with liquids?

**Keywords**  clear  cloudy  dissolve  insoluble  react
reaction  soluble  solution  suspension

**Let's think**

Not all solids behave in the same way when they are mixed with water or other liquids. Some solids dissolve, some don't, while other solids react when added to a liquid.

Does soil dissolve in water? Why?

## 👀 Let's explore!

SUGAR  SALT  PEPPER  FLOUR

- Which solid materials dissolve in water?
- Predict which solid materials dissolve in water and which don't.
- Test the materials to find out.
- What do you observe?
- Which mixtures have a clear and which have a cloudy appearance?
- Discuss and draw a conclusion.

 How do we identify if a solid dissolves in a liquid or not?

When a solid is added to a liquid and no chemical change happens, a mixture forms. If the solid is soluble in the liquid, it dissolves, and we cannot see it in its solid state. The mixture has a clear appearance and is called a solution.

If the solid is insoluble in the liquid, it doesn't dissolve, and we can see it in its solid state throughout the mixture. This type of mixture is called a suspension and has a cloudy appearance.

Why do labels on some liquid medicines say to shake the bottle well before taking the medicine?

 **Let's explore!**

- What happens when plaster of Paris is added to water?
- What happens when bicarbonate of soda is added to vinegar?
- Make predictions.
- Do the tests and record your observations.
- Discuss and draw conclusions.

(?) What are some ways to identify if a solid reacts with a liquid when it is added to the liquid?

There are some solids that when added to a liquid, don't mix but react with it. When two substances react, they join together and a new substance is formed. Most reactions are irreversible, as we cannot get the substances that reacted and joined together back. We recognise that a reaction takes place because we identify changes like the temperature increasing, bubbles forming, the colour changing, etc. Does the medicine tablet dissolve or react when it is put in water? Explain your answer.

- **When a solid is added to a liquid, the solid can mix or react with the liquid.**
- **Solids that mix with a liquid are soluble or insoluble in the liquid. Soluble solids form solutions and insoluble solids form suspensions.**
- **When a solid reacts with a liquid, they join together and a new substance is formed.**

# 2.4 How do saturated solutions form?

**Let's think**

When we mix a solid with a liquid, and the solid dissolves in the liquid, a solution is formed. The components of a solution are the solvent and the solute.

Can you dissolve as much sugar as you want in a cup of tea?

## Let's explore!

- Investigate if the amount of sugar that can dissolve in 100 ml of water is the same as the amount of salt that can dissolve in 100 ml of water.
- Make a prediction.
- Plan a fair test.
- Do the test and record your results.
- Discuss and draw a conclusion.

SUGAR    SALT

**?**  Is the amount of the solute that can dissolve in a given amount of water affected by the type of the solute?

**B**

A solution forms after a solid dissolves in a liquid. The substance that dissolves is the solute, and the liquid that the solute dissolves in is the solvent. When a liquid is mixed with a solid that is soluble in it, the particles of the liquid go between the particles of the solid. The solid solute dissolves, and it is no longer visible in its solid state. A specific volume of a liquid solvent can dissolve a specific amount of different solutes. When the solvent is not able to dissolve more of a solute, the solution becomes saturated. The more of a liquid solvent you have, the more solute can dissolve in it. The amount of a solute needed to dissolve and make a saturated solution is affected by the kind of substance the solute is.

Seawater is also a solution. Which is the solvent and which is one of the solutes in seawater?

 **What is another way of making a saturated solution without adding more of the solute to the solution?**

*Science in action*

In both cups of tea sugar was added, but of different amounts. How can you tell which cup of tea has a saturated solution?

- **The components of a solution are the solvent and the solute.**
- **The solid substance that dissolves is the solute, and the liquid that the solute dissolves into is the solvent.**
- **A solution is saturated when the solvent is not able to dissolve any more of the solute.**
- **The amount of a solute that can dissolve in a given amount of solvent is different for different solutes.**

# 2.5 Which factors affect the rate of dissolving?

Keywords  factor  follow a pattern  form  grain  stir

**Let's think**

When a solution forms, the solute that dissolves in the solvent can dissolve faster or slower. When the solid dissolves faster in the solvent, it has a high rate of dissolving. There are **factors** that affect the rate at which a solid dissolves.

**A**

1. Do you think that stirring can make sugar dissolve faster in tea?

2. What do you think affects the rate of dissolving?

## Let's explore!

- Investigate the factors that affect how fast a solid solute dissolves in a liquid solvent.
- Make predictions.
- Plan fair tests.
- Do the tests and record your results.
- Do your measurements follow a pattern?
- Discuss and draw conclusions.

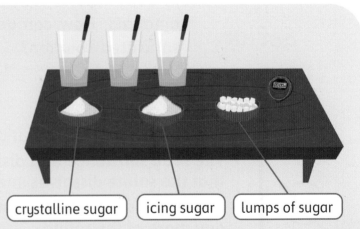

crystalline sugar   icing sugar   lumps of sugar

 What are the factors that affect the rate of dissolving of a solid in a liquid?

**B**

The factors that affect how fast a specific amount of a solid solute dissolves in specific amount of a liquid solvent are the temperature of the solvent, stirring and the grain size of the solid solute.

When the temperature of the solvent is high, its particles move fast, and can spread between the particles of the solute faster. This causes the solute to dissolve faster.

Stirring a solution also increases the rate of dissolving of a solid solute. When we stir a solution, we make the particles of the solute spread through the whole solution, helping the particles of the solvent to come into contact with more particles of the solute and go between them.

The size of the grains of a solid solute affects how fast it dissolves in a solvent. Different forms of sugar have a different rate of dissolving. Solids with a smaller grain size like icing sugar, dissolve a lot faster in water or other solvents, than solids with a larger grain size like the lumps of sugar.

1. Why do we usually use hot water to make coffee?

2. What can we do to make sugar dissolve faster in cold water?

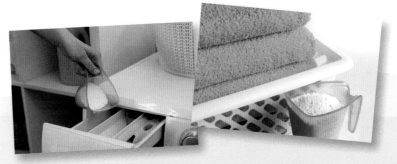

*Science in action*

Washing powder sometimes doesn't dissolve well in the washing machine when low water temperatures are used. Why is it better to wash the clothes in the washing machine with warm or hot water when washing powder is used?

- **The measure of how fast or slow a solute dissolves in a solvent to make a solution is called the rate of dissolving.**
- **The rate at which a solid solute dissolves, is affected by the temperature of the solvent, stirring and the grain size of the solid solute.**

# 2.6 How can we separate solids from liquids?

Keywords    *filter*    *filtration*

**Let's think**

**Mixing substances that don't react with each other is a reversible change. There are several ways through which we can separate these substances and get them back.**

Substances that are made of only one kind of particle are pure substances, like water that is made of only particles of water. The particles in a pure substance are joined together, and this is why we are not able to separate them. All kinds of mixtures, including solutions and suspensions, contain more than one substance, and are made of more than one kind of particle. The particles in a mixture, like the particles in seawater, are not joined and this is why we can separate them, and get the substances that were mixed together back. Name two pure substances and two mixtures.

 After a solid has dissolved in a liquid, we can no longer see it in its solid state.

**Let's explore!**

- Investigate how you can separate different solids from liquids.
- Do the tests and record your observations.
- Discuss and draw conclusions.

? When do you use filtration to separate solids from liquids and when do you use evaporation?

**B**

Solids that are insoluble in a liquid, don't dissolve when mixed with it, but form a mixture. To separate a liquid from a solid that is insoluble in it, we use filters. Filtration is a process similar to sieving. Smaller particles of the liquid pass through the tiny holes of the filter, while the larger grains of the insoluble solid cannot pass through, and stay in the filter. Solids that are soluble in a liquid, form a solution when mixed with it. We cannot separate the solid solute from the solvent through filtration. The whole solution can pass through the holes of a filter and we cannot collect the solid. To separate solutions we use evaporation and boiling through heating the solutions. In this way, only the liquid solvents evaporate and the solid solutes are left in their solid state.

How is filtration used to make coffee?

 **How can you separate a mixture of salt and sand?**

*Science in action*

Filters are also used to provide us with clean water. The filters that are used in houses, are devices that are filled with layers of substances like activated carbon, gravel and sand of different grain sizes. As the water passes through the filter, the insoluble dirt that may be in it cannot pass through the spaces between the grains of the sand and soil, and is separated from the water. How do you think harmful microorganisms which are very small in size and can pass through filters are cleaned from water?

- **A pure substance is made of only one kind of particle and the particles are joined together.**
- **A mixture has more than one kind of particle and the particles are not joined together and this is why we can separate them.**
- **We can separate insoluble solids from a liquid through filtration.**
- **We can separate soluble solids from a liquid through evaporation and boiling.**

# 2  Review

Go to the **Unit maps** section at the back of the book.

**1.** Match. Write **1** or **2** in the boxes.

> **1.** reversible change   **2.** irreversible change

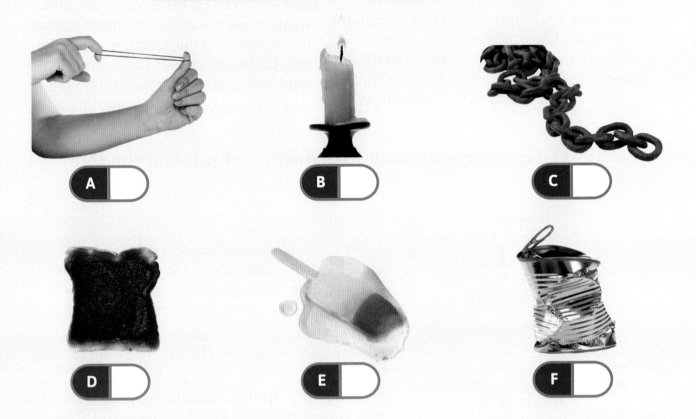

**A**   **B**   **C**

**D**   **E**   **F**

**2.** Read the sentences. Write **Yes** or **No**.

**1.** Sugar dissolves faster in cold water than in hot water. _____

**2.** Mixtures in the solid state form when we mix solid materials without a chemical change taking place. _____

**3.** Suspensions have a clear appearance. _____

**4.** No more solute can dissolve in a saturated solution. _____

**5.** Some ways of separating solid mixtures are using a magnet and separating by hand. _____

**6.** Insoluble solids form solutions when added to water. _____

**7.** The same amount of any substance can dissolve in a given amount of water. _____

**8.** Stirring makes a solid solute dissolve faster in a liquid solvent. _____

**3.** Tick (✔) what happens when each material is added in water. Then answer the questions.

| Material | It dissolves when added to water | It doesn't dissolve when added to water | It reacts with water |
|---|---|---|---|
| Salt | | | |
| Rice | | | |
| Plaster of Paris | | | |
| Sugar | | | |
| Sand | | | |
| Medicine tablet | | | |

**1.** Which materials form a solution when added to water? Explain your answer.

_____

_____

_____

**2.** Which materials can you get back through filtration or sieving? Explain your answer.

_____

_____

_____

**3.** Through which process can you separate salt or sugar from water? Explain your answer.

_____

_____

_____

**4.** Can you get the medicine tablet back after it is added to water? Explain your answer.

_____

_____

 # Feeding Relationships

## 3.1 What are producers and consumers?

**Keywords**
aquatic   consumer   glucose   photosynthesis
phytoplankton   producer   species   starch
zooplankton

 **Let's think**   All species need energy to grow. Energy is stored in food.

Plants produce their own food through photosynthesis, and are called producers. Photosynthesis happens in the green parts of plants. The plants' food is called glucose. Plants use light energy from the Sun, water and carbon dioxide, to produce glucose and oxygen. Some glucose is used for plant growth, while the rest is stored in the plant as starch. Animals that eat plants get energy from the starch that is stored in the plants.

What else do animals use that is produced by plants? What do they use it for?

A

B

C

Animals cannot make their own food. They have to eat plants or other animals to get energy. Animals are called consumers. What are the animals eating in the pictures?

## 👀 Let's explore!

- Investigate if plants can make food without light.
- Make predictions.
- Do the test and record your observations.
- Discuss and draw a conclusion.

(?) Can plants make their food without getting light? Why?

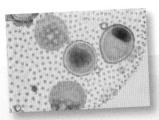

*Science in action*

In aquatic habitats there are very small kinds of living things called phytoplankton that make their own food through photosynthesis. There are also small kinds of living things called zooplankton. Phytoplankton are eaten by zooplankton. Are phytoplankton and zooplankton producers or consumers?

- **Plants make their own food through photosynthesis, and are called producers.**
- **Photosynthesis happens in the green parts of plants only when they are able to get light, water and carbon dioxide.**
- **Animals eat plants or other animals, and are called consumers.**

# 3.2 What are food chains?

**Keywords**    arrow   depend on   feeding relationship
              food chain   write down

**Let's think**

The habitat of a species is the area it lives in, as well as the climate, the other non-living things and the species that exist there. There are producers and consumers in a habitat. In a habitat, there are feeding relationships between living things. Living things depend on each other.

**A**

What feeding relationships do you recognise in the lake habitat?

**B**

| corn | mouse | snake | owl |

**B**

A food chain depicts the feeding relationships between different species. Food chains always begin with the producers. The arrows in food chains show which living thing is eaten by which. Describe the feeding relationships shown in the food chain.

> **!** Phytoplankton are the producers in aquatic habitats.

## 👀 Let's explore!

- Search for information about feeding relationships in a habitat.
- Look in books or on the Internet.
- Write down a food chain of this habitat.
- Present your findings to the class.

**?** What are the parts of a food chain?

 **Science in action**

Sharks eat seals and seals eat fish. Fish eat zooplankton and zooplankton eat phytoplankton. What will happen to sharks if there are no phytoplankton in the aquatic habitats?

 Write down two food chains that include humans.

- **Food chains show the feeding relationships in a habitat.**
- **Food chains always begin with producers.**

# 3.3 What are food webs?

Keywords    food web    population

**Let's think**

Living things can eat and can be eaten by more than one living thing. There are many different food chains in a habitat.

**A**

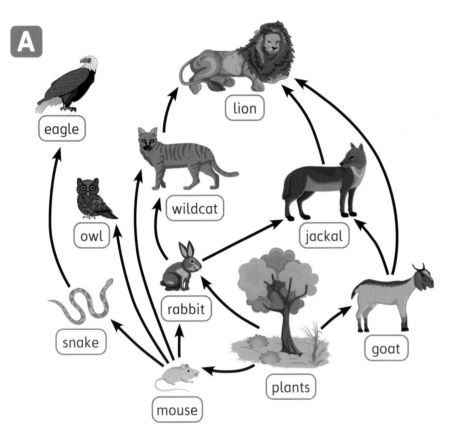

We draw food webs to show the feeding relationships between the species of a habitat. Food webs are made up of two or more food chains. All the food chains of a food web begin with the producers. The arrows in the food chains of a food web show which living thing is eaten by which.

1. What is eaten by lions?
2. Write down the food chains that include the goat.
3. Write down the food chains that include the wildcat.

## Let's explore!

- Search for information about feeding relationships in a habitat.
- Look in books or on the Internet.
- Create a food web for this habitat.
- Present your findings to the class.

**?** What information does a food web show?

**B**

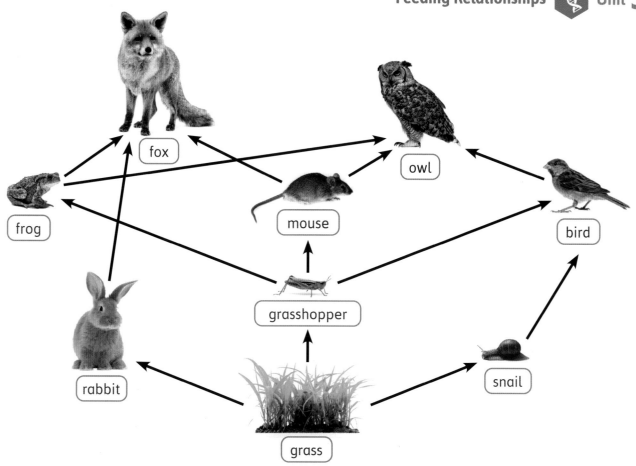

Food webs show us how living things depend on each other. Do the frog and mice populations depend on the snail population?

Science in action

Pandas mostly eat bamboo. What will most likely happen if bamboo is taken from their habitats?

- **A species may be part of different food chains in a habitat.**
- **Food webs are diagrams that show many feeding relationships between the species in a habitat.**

# 3.4 What is a predator and what is a prey?

**Keywords** *explore hunt predator prey*

**Let's think**

There are animals that eat only plants, there are animals that eat only other animals, and there are animals that eat both plants and animals.

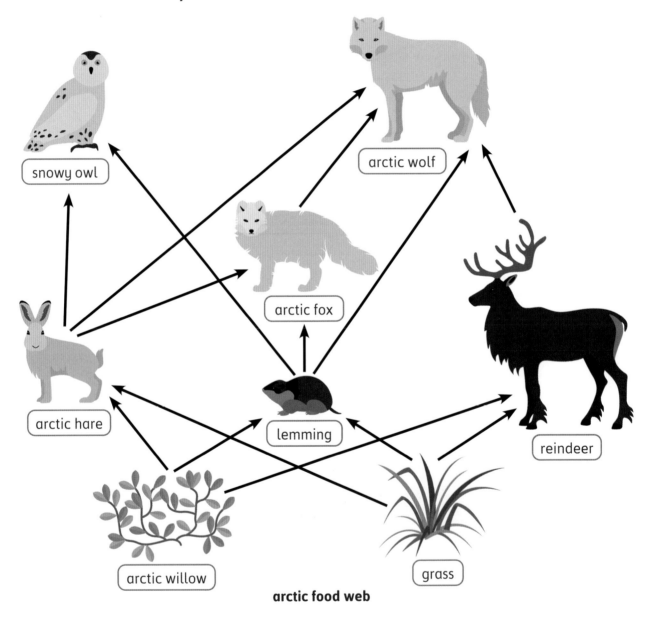

**arctic food web**

Predators are animals that hunt other animals for food. The animals that predators hunt are called prey.

1. Which animals in the food web are predators and which are prey?

2. Which animal in the food web is both a predator and prey?

##  Let's explore!

- Explore your school playground, looking for feeding relationships.
- Observe an animal.
- What does it eat?
- What is its predator?
- Write down the food chain that this animal is a part of.

 What are the animals after the producers in a food chain, and what are the animals that are last?

 Are humans predators?

*Science in action*

All species have to adapt to their habitat to survive, like the arctic wolf and the arctic hare. How do the characteristics of prey and their predators help them survive in their habitat?

- **Predators are animals that hunt and eat other animals.**
- **Animals that are hunted and eaten by predators are prey.**

# 3 Review

Go to the **Unit maps** section at the back of the book.

1. **Read the text. Draw arrows (→) to create a food web to show the feeding relationships between the living things. Then answer the question.**

   Phytoplankton are eaten by zooplankton. Zooplankton are eaten by penguins, cod and squid. Leopard seals eat penguins, cod and squid. Orca whales are only predators and hunt penguins, leopard seals and squid.

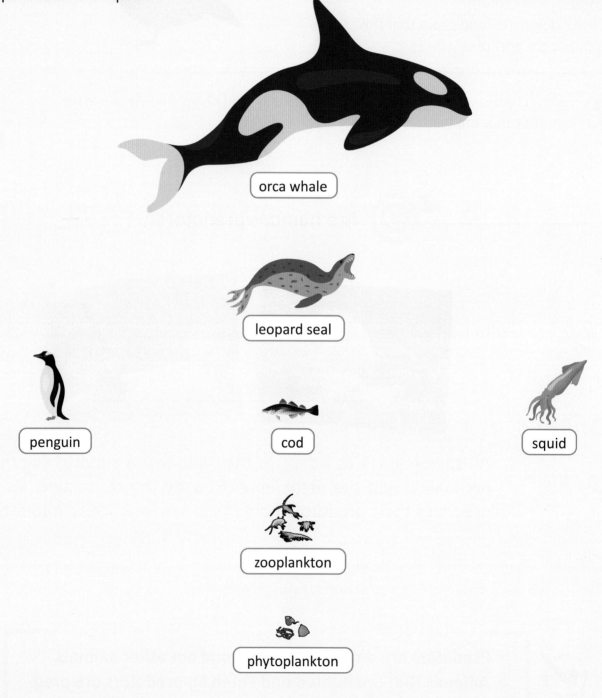

orca whale

leopard seal

penguin

cod

squid

zooplankton

phytoplankton

The population of zooplankton decreases. Does the population of orca whales depend on the population of zooplankton? How?

**2.** Look at the pictures of different species. Draw arrows (→) to make a food chain. Then answer the questions.

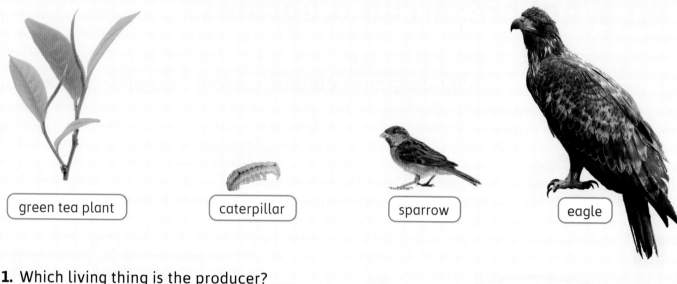

green tea plant          caterpillar          sparrow          eagle

**1.** Which living thing is the producer? _____

**2.** Which living thing is only a predator? _____

**3.** Which living thing is only prey? _____

**4.** Which living thing is both a predator and prey? _____

**3.** Read the sentences. Write **Yes** or **No**.

**1.** Humans are part of many food chains. _____

**2.** All of the glucose produced by plants is used for their growth. _____

**3.** Some kinds of small living things, like phytoplankton, are producers. _____

**4.** Photosynthesis also happens when plants are not able to get light. _____

**5.** Food chains always begin with a consumer. _____

**6.** Plants make their own food through the process of photosynthesis. _____

**7.** Plants release carbon dioxide into the air through the process of photosynthesis. _____

**8.** Plants use light energy from the Sun, carbon dioxide from the air and water from the soil to produce glucose. _____

# 4 ⚛ Electricity

## 4.1 What are circuit diagrams?

Keywords    circuit diagram    electric current    go off    symbol

**Let's think**

A circuit is a path which an **electric current** passes through. A circuit is made up of a cell or battery and other components, like wires, bulbs and switches.

**A**

How are the pictures of the circuits different?

**B**

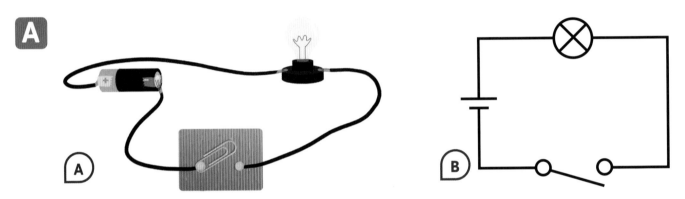

| | | |
|---|---|---|
| | cell | ⊣⊢ |
| | battery | ⊣⊦⊢ |
| | wire | — |
| | bulb | ⊗ |
| | open switch | ◦⟋◦ |
| | closed switch | ◦—◦ |
| | motor | Ⓜ |
| | buzzer | ⏚ |

We draw circuit diagrams to show a circuit. There is a symbol for each component in a circuit.

Why do we use symbols to draw circuit diagrams?

## Let's explore!

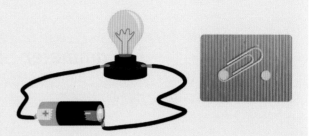

- Investigate where you have to put the switch in a simple circuit so that the light bulb goes off.
- Make a prediction.
- Draw circuit diagrams of the circuits you will test.
- Record your observations.
- Discuss and draw a conclusion.

 How are switches used in a circuit?

**A**

- Investigate how you will connect two cells to make the bulb in a simple circuit light up.
- Make a prediction.
- Test your circuit.
- Reverse one cell and test the circuit again.
- Record your observations.
- Discuss and draw a conclusion.

 How should cells be connected to make a circuit work?

**B**

*Science in action*

Batteries are made of cells. Each cell is 1.5 V. How do we draw a car battery and how do we draw a battery made of three cells connected one after the other with symbols?

- **Circuit symbols show the components of a circuit.**
- **Circuit diagrams show how the components are connected in a circuit.**
- **We can break a circuit using a switch.**
- **The opposite terminals of cells should be connected to make a circuit work.**

# 4.2 How do we measure the size of an electric current?

Keywords: ammeter   ampere (A)   electrical energy   energy source

**Let's think**

An energy source, like a cell or a battery, causes the particles in a complete circuit to flow around. This flow is the electric current.

1. How do you know that there is an electric current in the circuit?

2. The cell provides the circuit with electrical energy that causes the particles to flow around the circuit. An electric current carries the energy to the components of the circuit. How does the bulb change the electrical energy?

---

(A)

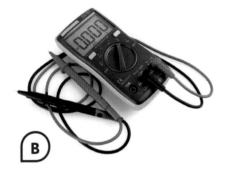

(B)

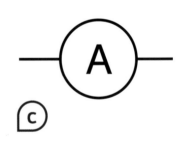

(C)

The number of particles passing any point in a circuit each second is a measure of the electric current. We use an ammeter or a multimeter to measure the size of the electric current. The unit of electric current is the ampere (A).

How does the number of particles passing a point in a circuit affect the size of an electric current?

 **Let's explore!**

- Investigate if the electric current decreases as it passes through a simple circuit.
- Make predictions.
- Connect an ammeter in different positions in a simple circuit.
- Record your measurements.
- Discuss and draw a conclusion.

 Does the electric current decrease as it passes through a simple circuit?

How will two of the same bulbs connected one after the other in a circuit shine?

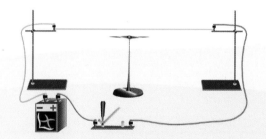 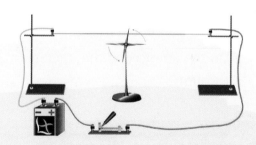

*Science in action*

In 1820, Hans Christian Oersted discovered that electric current in a wire made a compass needle change direction. What force does the electric current put on the compass needle?

- **We measure the size of an electric current in a circuit with an ammeter.**
- **The unit of electric current is the ampere (A).**
- **The size of an electric current is the same all around a simple circuit.**
- **The electric current flows in one direction around a simple circuit.**

# 4.3 How do the length and thickness of a wire affect the brightness of a bulb?

**Keywords**   *length   repeat   thick   thickness*

**Let's think**

An electric current passes through thin and short wires in the circuits you made. Electrical energy comes to our homes and buildings through thick and long wires that are held by pylons high above the ground.

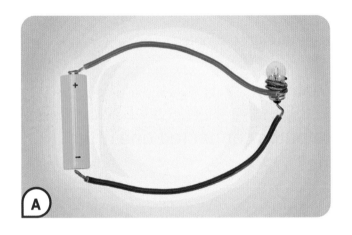

A

B

Do the length and the thickness of a wire affect the amount of electric current passing through?

## Let's explore!

- Investigate how the length of the wire affects the electric current passing through a circuit.
- Make a prediction.
- Measure the electric current in the circuit.
- Repeat for different lengths of wire.
- Record your measurements.
- Discuss and draw a conclusion.

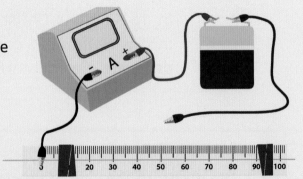

**?** How does the length of the wire affect the electric current passing through a circuit?

A

## ᐁᐁ Let's explore!

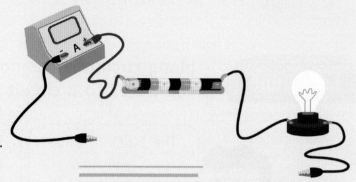

- Investigate how the thickness of the wire affects the electric current passing through a circuit.
- Make a prediction.
- Observe the brightness of the bulb.
- Measure the electric current in the circuit.
- Repeat for wires of different thickness.
- Record your measurements.
- Discuss and draw a conclusion.

1. How does the thickness of the wire affect the electric current passing through a circuit?
2. How does the bulb shine in relation to the size of the electric current that passes through it?

**B**

*Science in action*

Dimmer switches have a long resistance wire inside. You can change the length of this wire by turning the switch. How does a dimmer switch work?

- **The shorter and the thicker a wire is, the more electric current passes through it.**
- **A bulb will shine more brightly when there is more electric current passing through it.**

# 4.4 How do we connect bulbs in a circuit?

**Keywords**  *in parallel*   *in series*   *parallel circuit*   *series circuit*

**Let's think**   Many circuits have more than one bulb. The bulbs can be connected to a circuit in two ways.

The bulbs in both circuits will have the same brightness.

The bulbs that are closer to the negative terminal of the cell will shine more brightly.

Enzo made a circuit where the electric current has only one path to pass through. He made a series circuit. Samir made a circuit where the electric current can pass through more than one path. Some of the electric current passes through the one bulb and some passes through the other bulb. He made a parallel circuit.

Do you agree with Enzo and Samir?

 The more electric current that passes through a bulb, the more brightly it shines.

## 👀 Let's explore!

- Investigate how the brightness of the bulbs changes as you add more bulbs in series.
- Make predictions.
- Create the circuits.
- Observe the brightness of the bulbs in each circuit.
- Measure the electric current in each circuit.
- Discuss and draw a conclusion.

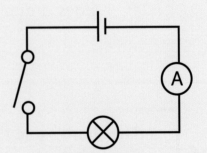

(?)  How does the brightness of the bulbs change as you add more bulbs in series?

A

What will happen if you unscrew one of the bulbs connected in a series circuit?

## 👀 Let's explore!

- Investigate how the brightness of the bulbs changes as you add more bulbs in parallel.
- Make predictions.
- Create the circuits.
- Observe the brightness of the bulbs in each circuit.
- Discuss and draw a conclusion.

 1. How does the brightness of the bulbs change as you add more bulbs in parallel?

2. How do the bulbs in the series circuit shine compared to the same bulbs in the parallel circuit?

**B**

*Science in action*

Are the electrical appliances in our houses connected in series or in parallel? Why do you think that is?

- **Adding more bulbs in series to a circuit causes them to shine less brightly.**
- **Adding more bulbs in parallel to a circuit will not affect their brightness.**
- **Connecting the bulbs in parallel causes them to shine more brightly than connecting them in series.**

# 4.5 What happens when we add more cells in a circuit?

**Keywords**   label   properly   volt (V)   voltage

 **Let's think**   Many circuits need more than one cell to make their components work.

 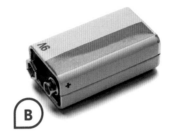 

The voltage of a battery or cell is a measure of the amount of electrical energy the battery or cell provides to the circuit. The voltage is written on each battery or cell. We measure the voltage in units, called volts (V).

Each cell is 1.5 V. If cells are connected one after another to make a battery, the voltages of all the cells are added together.

What is the voltage of each battery or cell in the pictures?

---

**B**

**A** 6 V motor

**B** 3 V buzzer

**C** 1.5 V bulb

Each component is labelled with a number of volts. The number of volts on each component shows us how many volts each component needs to work properly.

1. What should the voltage of the battery connected to each component be?

2. How many 1.5 V cells does each component need to work properly?

 Connect the opposite ends of the cells together to make a more powerful battery.

##  Let's explore!

- Investigate how the brightness of a bulb changes as you add more cells in a simple circuit.
- Make predictions.
- Create the circuits.
- Observe the brightness of the bulb.
- Measure the electric current in each circuit.
- Discuss and draw a conclusion.

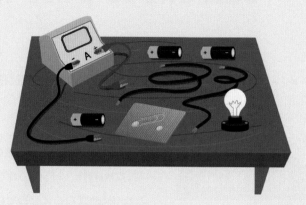

**?** How does the brightness of the bulb change as you add more cells in a simple circuit?

**A**

- Investigate how adding more cells in a circuit affects the way a component works.
- Make predictions.
- Change the number of cells in the circuit.
- Record your observations.
- Discuss and draw a conclusion.

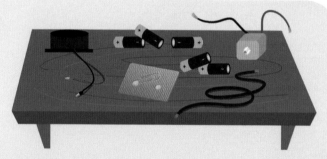

**?** How do different components work when you add more cells in the circuit?

**B**

*Science in action*

1. How many volts does the camera need to work?

2. A remote control needs 3 V to work properly and a washing machine needs 110 V or 220 V to work properly. What energy source is best to use for each device?

- **Adding more cells in a simple circuit causes the electric current to increase.**
- **Adding more cells in a circuit causes a bulb to shine more brightly, a buzzer to make a louder sound and a motor to turn faster.**

# 4.6 Do all materials allow an electric current to pass through them?

**Keywords**  distilled water   electrical conductor   electrical insulator

**Let's think**

An electric current always needs a complete path to pass through. The path has to be made of materials that allow an electric current to pass through.

**A**

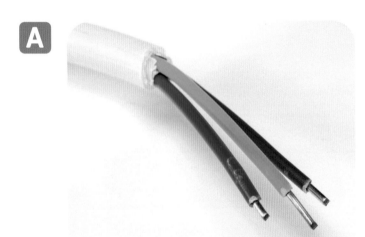

The wires are made of copper covered with rubber or plastic. Why are these materials used?

## 👓 Let's explore!

- Which materials allow an electric current to pass through them?
- Make predictions.
- Test some objects made of different materials.
- Record your results.
- Sort the materials into groups.
- Discuss and draw a conclusion.

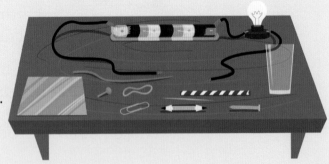

**(?)** Which materials are electrical conductors and which are electrical insulators?

**B**

Tap water is a solution of water and salts dissolved in it. Why do we usually put distilled water in our steam irons instead of tap water?

 ## Let's explore!

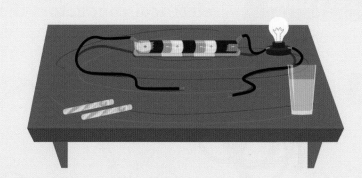

- Does water allow an electric current to pass through it?
- Make predictions.
- Test distilled water and water with salt dissolved in it.
- Record your results.
- Discuss and draw a conclusion.

**?** Is water an electrical conductor or an electrical insulator?

**B**

Do you think our body is an electrical conductor or an electrical insulator, knowing that it contains about 65% water?

*Science in action*

 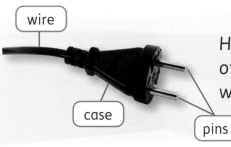

wire

case

pins

How are the materials of the plug and the wall socket used?

✓
- **Electrical conductors are materials that allow an electric current to pass through them.**
- **Electrical insulators are materials that don't allow an electric current to pass through them.**
- **Distilled water is an electrical insulator, but water with salts dissolved in it is an electrical conductor.**

# 4.7 Are some metals better electrical conductors than others?

**Let's think**

Metals are electrical conductors. But some metals are better electrical conductors than others.

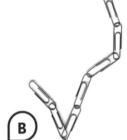

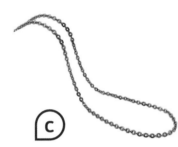

1. Can you put steel paper clips or a golden necklace in place of the copper wires in a circuit?

2. Would there be any difference in the circuit?

**!** Alloys are solid mixtures of materials, at least one of which is a metal.

## 👀 Let's explore!

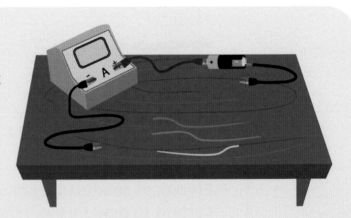

- Investigate which metal conducts the most electric current.
- Make predictions.
- Plan a fair test.
- Test some wires made of different metals.
- Record your results.
- Discuss and draw a conclusion.

**?** Do all metals conduct the same amount of electric current?

**B**

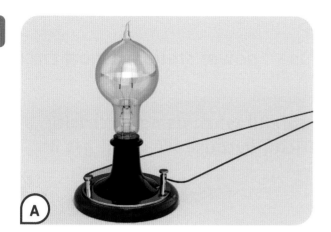

A

B

Many scientists helped in the development of the light bulb. The first light bulb in the early 19th century had a copper filament. Later, platinum was used for the filament which shone for a longer time than copper, but platinum was too expensive.

Thomas Edison improved the light bulb by making a bulb that was cheap and shone for a long time. He tested many different materials for the filament and decided on carbon. He found out that the material

for the filament needs to both burn for as long as possible and be as thin as possible. Thomas Edison knew that the best material for the filament was tungsten, the metal that has the highest melting point, but he couldn't make tungsten thin enough to use in a bulb until 1910.

1. What common property do copper, platinum and carbon have?

2. Why should the filament have a high melting point?

*Science in action*

Silver is a better electrical conductor than copper. Why are wires not made of silver?

- **Metals are electrical conductors.**
- **Some metals are better electrical conductors than others.**

# 4.8 How do we use electricity safely?

Keywords  effect   electric shock   fuse   power station   short circuit

**Let's think**

We should always be careful when using electricity, especially mains electricity because we could get an electric shock.

A

B

Power stations produce electrical energy that is carried by electric current to our homes and buildings through cables.

1. How are electrical conductors and insulators used in picture A?

2. Why is the man working on the pylon wearing rubber gloves and shoes with rubber soles?

A

25 7

B

1. A lot of electrical appliances work with mains electricity. When you plug an appliance into a wall socket of your house you complete a big circuit from your house to the power station and back again. What is the voltage of the mains electricity in picture A?

2. An electric current may not travel through the correct path when it finds a shorter path to travel. This is when a short circuit happens. What will happen to the woman in picture B?

! Electrical energy carried by an electric current can be changed into heat in different components of a circuit.

## 👀 Let's explore!

- Investigate the effects of a short circuit.
- What will happen if you bring the two paper clips together?
- Do the test and record your observations.
- Discuss and draw a conclusion.

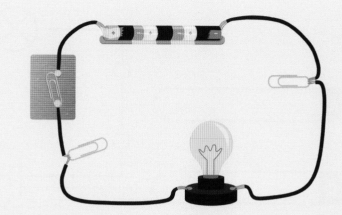

(?) What are the effects of a short circuit?

*Science in action*

1. A fuse is a device with a thin metal wire inside that prevents short circuits. How does a fuse work?

2. Why should we never touch electrical appliances with wet hands?

- **Mains electricity has a high voltage and can be very dangerous.**
- **We have to use electricity safely.**
- **A short circuit can cause fires and electric shocks.**
- **We should never touch wires that are not covered by an electrical insulator.**
- **We should never have wet hands or feet when using electricity.**

1. Look at the picture. Write the names of the components in boxes A-D. Then answer the questions.

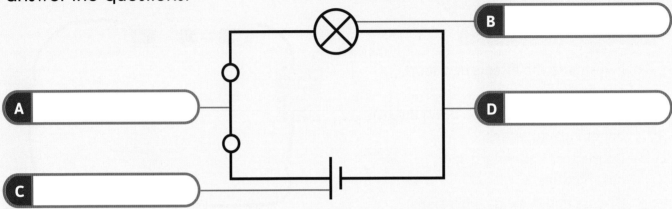

A

B

C

D

1. What is this drawing known as? Circle. **ray diagram / circuit diagram**

2. What can you add to the circuit to measure the electric current passing through? Circle. **ammeter / buzzer**

3. What is the unit of electric current? Circle. **ampere / volt**

4. How can you change the circuit to make the bulb shine more brightly? Circle. **I can use a longer wire. / I can use a thicker wire**.

2. Tick (✔) the electrical conductors.

**1.** copper

**2.** plastic

**3.** sea water

**4.** graphite

**5.** wood

**6.** aluminium

**7.** rubber

**8.** distilled water

**3.** Match the circuit diagrams with the sentences. Write **1-3** in the boxes.

**1.** The bulbs will not light up.
**2.** The bulbs will shine more brightly.
**3.** The bulbs will shine less brightly.

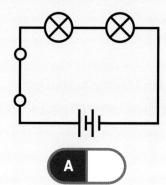
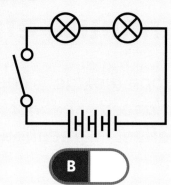
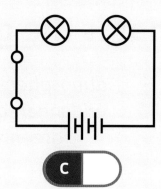

A     B     C

**4.** Look at the circuit diagrams. Then answer the questions.

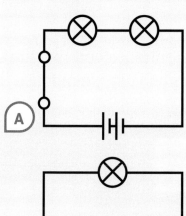

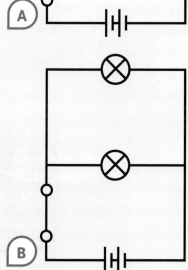

**1.** How will the bulbs in circuit A shine? Tick (✔), and explain your answer.

   **a.** The bulbs will shine with the same brightness.

   **b.** The one bulb will shine more brightly than the other.

**2.** How do the bulbs in circuit A shine compared to the same bulbs in circuit B?

_____

_____

_____

_____

_____

**5.** Look at the signs. Then answer the questions.

Do not touch electrical appliances or wires with wet hands.

Do not touch damaged wires.

**1.** Why is it dangerous to use an electrical appliance with wet hands?

**2.** Why is it dangerous to touch damaged wires?

# 5 Humans and the Environment

## 5.1 What is the greenhouse effect?

**Keywords**
atmosphere    carbon dioxide    coal    deforestation
endangered    enhanced    extinct    global warming
greenhouse effect    greenhouse gas    loss

**Let's think**

People's actions affect the environment in good and bad ways. When something harmful is added to the environment, it causes pollution.

 The light energy from the Sun warms the inside of a greenhouse and the plastic or glass, that the greenhouse is made of, keeps the warmth in the greenhouse.

**A**

A) **natural greenhouse effect**

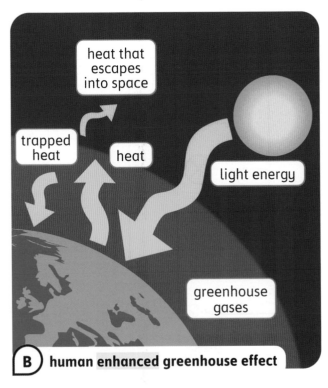

B) **human enhanced greenhouse effect**

The Sun sends light energy towards the Earth. Some of the light energy of the Sun passes through the atmosphere and warms the surface of the Earth. The surface of the Earth then releases heat into the atmosphere. Some of this heat escapes into space, but some gets trapped by some gases in the atmosphere keeping the Earth warm. This is the natural greenhouse effect that keeps temperatures on the Earth at levels that allow living things to survive.

Gases in the atmosphere, like carbon dioxide and water vapour, that trap some of the heat from the Sun are called greenhouse gases.

Human actions can increase the amount of greenhouse gases in the atmosphere. Burning fuels, like coal and oil, adds carbon dioxide to the atmosphere, causing the human enhanced greenhouse effect. As the greenhouse gases increase, they trap more heat which increases the temperatures of the Earth, causing global warming.

What is the difference between the natural greenhouse effect and the human enhanced greenhouse effect?

 **Let's explore!**

- Investigate how the temperature of the atmosphere is affected as carbon dioxide increases.
- Make predictions.
- Do the test and record your results.
- Discuss and draw a conclusion.

 How is the temperature of the atmosphere affected as carbon dioxide increases?

**B**

A

B

1. Deforestation happens when people cut down a large number of trees in forests. What are the reasons for deforestation?

2. One of the results of deforestation is the loss of the habitats of many species around the world. The loss of habitats often causes animals and plants that live there to become endangered or extinct, like the Bengal tigers. Why does this happen?

- **The greenhouse effect keeps the Earth warm for living things to survive.**
- **The actions of humans cause the human enhanced greenhouse effect by increasing the amount of greenhouse gases in the atmosphere.**
- **Global warming happens because of the human enhanced greenhouse effect.**
- **Deforestation causes many species to lose their habitats.**

# 5.2 How do we pollute the atmosphere?

**Keywords**  *acid rain*  *activity*  *damage*

**Let's think**

Human **activities** can harm the environment. The burning of fuels releases pollutants into the atmosphere.

A

B

Cars, lorries and buses burn fuels to move. Power stations burn fuels to produce electrical energy and factories burn fuels to produce different kinds of things. The burning

of different fuels produces fumes and smoke that have harmful gases.

How does air pollution affect our health?

## 👓 Let's explore!

- How can we reduce air pollution?
- Look in books or on the Internet.
- Make a poster to present your findings to your class.

 What are some ways to reduce air pollution?

A

**B**

Burning fuels releases harmful gases into the atmosphere. These gases react with water and oxygen in the atmosphere, and form new substances that fall to the ground mixed with rain, snow, fog or hail. This is called acid rain. The wind can move these gases long distances away from where they are released before they form acid rain. Acid rain can harm plants and animals, and damage buildings made from materials like limestone.

Is acid rain a problem only in areas where harmful gases are released?

 Chalk and marble are types of limestone.

##  Let's explore!

- Investigate if acid rain affects limestone.
- Make predictions.
- Do the test and record your observations.
- Discuss and draw a conclusion.

**?** How does acid rain affect limestone?

**B**

##  Do only humans' actions pollute the air?

*Science in action*

Marble was often used for statues and temples. The Caryatids are statues that were once standing at the temple of Acropolis. In 2009, the statues were removed from the temple and are now in the Acropolis Museum. Why are some parts of ancient buildings, like the Caryatids, moved inside a museum?

- **Air pollution affects human health.**
- **Burning fuels releases harmful gases into the atmosphere.**
- **Acid rain harms living things and damages buildings made of limestone.**
- **We can reduce air pollution by burning less fuels.**

# 5.3 How does our waste affect the environment?

Keywords  disposal   landfill site   microplastics   positive   recycling

**Let's think**  People produce waste in their everyday lives. They throw away leftovers, plastic bottles, glass jars, devices, etc.

**A**

The waste we throw away is collected and taken to landfill sites. Landfill sites are the most common areas of waste disposal. There, the waste is buried in the ground. The food and garden waste decay and release greenhouse gases into the atmosphere.

1. How does recycling affect waste disposal?

2. How does making compost with food and garden waste affect the environment?

**B**

A

B

Plastic waste stays in the environment for many years. Sometimes, plastic waste breaks into very small pieces called microplastics. These pieces harm species that live in the sea, like fish and shellfish, because they look like food.

How can we reduce plastic waste?

## Let's explore!

- Search for information about recycling different materials.
- Look in books or on the Internet.
- Make a poster to present your findings to your class.

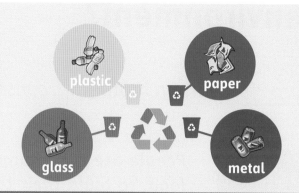

**(?)** What are the positive effects of recycling?

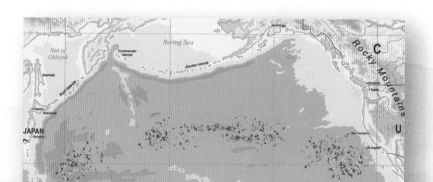

*Science in action*

There are five areas in the ocean, called garbage patches, where plastic waste collects naturally because ocean water flows in a circular pattern. The plastic waste can be large like a fishing net, but most of it is microplastics. That's why we cannot see the patches with the naked eye, or observe them by plane or satellite. Garbage patches are very big, and it is very difficult to remove them from the oceans. What can we do to prevent the plastic waste from entering the oceans?

- **Recycling, reusing and reducing have positive effects on the environment.**
- **Making compost with food and garden waste reduces the amount of greenhouse gases in the atmosphere.**
- **Plastic waste may break into smaller pieces and affect species that live in the sea.**

# 5.4 How do our activities affect the environment?

Keywords    carbon footprint    conservation area    negative    suggest

**Let's think**

People use the ground to get different materials, to grow food, to build their towns, etc.

marble quarry

People get different types of rocks from quarries. Marble is a type of limestone that people use to make buildings.

What negative effects do quarries have on the environment?

A

B

C

People get everything they need to eat from farms, e.g. vegetables, milk, meat, etc. The energy that these farms use every day increases the amount of greenhouse gases in the atmosphere.

When we use electrical energy, drive our car, use public transport or throw away our waste, greenhouse gases are released. The carbon footprint is the amount of greenhouse gases that all the activities of a person, a company, a country, etc. produce. When you leave a room and you don't turn the lights off, when you drive your car a lot or when you send all of your waste to the landfill site, you increase your carbon footprint.

Why do these activities increase your carbon footprint?

**Let's explore!**

- How can you reduce your carbon footprint?
- Look in books or on the Internet.
- Make a poster to present your findings to your class.

**(?)** What are some ways to reduce your carbon footprint?

 **C**

Humans can also do a lot of things to protect the environment and prevent the loss of habitats. A human activity that has a positive effect on the environment is to create protected or conservation areas. These areas are protected by governments against actions that may change them, e.g. deforestation, or harming the life of the species that live there.

The Ross Sea Marine Protected Area in Antarctica is one of the largest conservation areas in the world. Scientists study the environment of the Ross Sea. It has species that are not found in any other place around the world, and food chains that are very important for the Antarctic environment.

Find out about other conservation areas around the world.

*Science in action*

Energy is needed to clean, heat and pump water to houses and buildings. The amount of water we use affects our carbon footprint.
Suggest ways to reduce the carbon footprint that comes from using water.

- **Quarries and farms have negative effects on the environment.**
- **Reducing our carbon footprint and creating conservation areas have a positive effect on the environment.**

# 5.5 How do we use natural resources as energy sources?

**Keywords**

advantage    conserve    crude oil    disadvantage
fossil fuel    natural gas    non-renewable
renewable    resource    solar panel    wind turbine

**Let's think**

Since prehistoric times, humans have been using natural resources to survive and make different objects.

Natural resources are things that exist in nature, like air, water, soil, plants and animals. Some natural resources, like air and water, are needed for life. Many natural resources, like coal and wind, are used to produce energy. Others, like plants and rocks, are used to make different objects.

What is the natural resource that is used as an energy source in the picture?

**B**

**A** coal mine

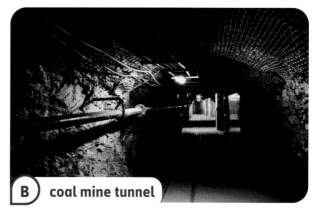
**B** coal mine tunnel

**C** crude oil and natural gas platform

**D** pumping crude oil to the surface

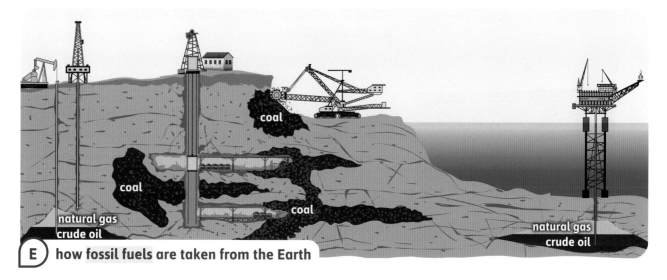
**E** how fossil fuels are taken from the Earth

Fossil fuels formed millions of years ago from decaying living things that were buried in the ground. Crude oil, natural gas and coal are fossil fuels. Most of the electrical energy we use comes from burning fossil fuels in power stations. Engineers drill in areas with coal, crude oil and natural gas to take them out of the Earth. Coal can be taken both from close to the surface of the Earth and from deep within the Earth. Crude oil and natural gas are often found in the same place deep within the Earth. To get crude oil and natural gas we need to pump them to bring them to the surface.

How does taking fossil fuels out of the Earth affect the environment?

A coal

B crude oil

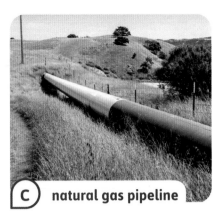

C natural gas pipeline

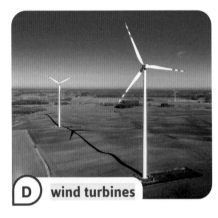

D wind turbines

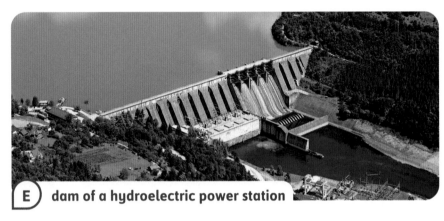

E dam of a hydroelectric power station

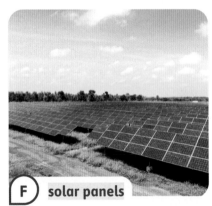

F solar panels

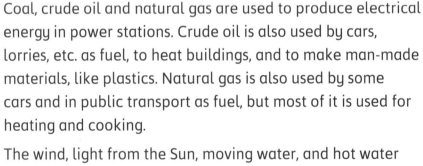

G power station that works using steam and hot water

Natural resources can be sorted into renewable resources and non-renewable resources. Renewable resources are quickly replaced by nature, but non-renewable resources cannot be replaced by nature in a short time.

Coal, crude oil and natural gas are used to produce electrical energy in power stations. Crude oil is also used by cars, lorries, etc. as fuel, to heat buildings, and to make man-made materials, like plastics. Natural gas is also used by some cars and in public transport as fuel, but most of it is used for heating and cooking.

The wind, light from the Sun, moving water, and hot water and steam from inside the Earth can also be used to produce electrical energy. Solar panels are also used to heat water. Hot water and steam from inside the Earth can also be used to heat homes or buildings.

Which of these natural resources are renewable resources and which of them are non-renewable resources?

## 👀 Let's explore!

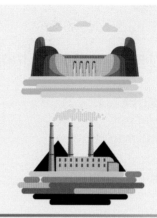

- Search for information about natural resources as energy sources.
- What are the advantages and disadvantages of using each natural resource as an energy source?
- Look in books or on the Internet.
- Make a poster to present your findings to your class.

1. What are the advantages and disadvantages of using non-renewable resources?
2. What are the advantages and disadvantages of using renewable resources?

A

B

We can take care of the environment by conserving energy and natural resources so that they will last longer. That way, we can reduce the negative effects of using natural resources as energy sources, on the environment. What can we do to conserve energy and natural resources?

*Science in action*

Iceland produces up to 20% of its electrical energy using steam and hot water from inside the Earth. Find other uses of steam and hot water from inside the Earth as energy sources.

- **Natural resources are used as energy sources.**
- **Natural resources are sorted into non-renewable and renewable resources.**
- **Renewable resources that are used as energy sources are less harmful to the environment than non-renewable resources.**
- **We can take care of the environment by conserving energy and natural resources.**

1. Draw lines to match the two parts of each sentence.

   **1.** Quarries

   **2.** Global warming

   **3.** Carbon footprint

   **4.** Landfill sites

   **5.** Conservation areas

   happens because of the enhanced greenhouse effect.

   protect the habitats of many species.

   are places of waste disposal.

   produce a lot of noise that causes animals to leave their habitats.

   is a measure of the greenhouse gases produced by different activities.

2. Look at the picture. Then answer the questions.

   **1.** What fossil fuel is taken from the Earth in the picture?

   **2.** How does this activity affect the environment?

   **3.** What negative effects does using fossil fuels as energy sources have on the environment?

   **4.** What can we do to reduce the use of fossil fuels?

3. Read the sentences. Write **Yes** or **No**.

   **1.** The greenhouse effect is important for living things. _____

   **2.** Deforestation helps to reduce the amount of carbon dioxide in the atmosphere. _____

   **3.** We can reduce our carbon footprint by using renewable resources as energy sources. _____

   **4.** Reducing our carbon footprint means more greenhouse gases are released into the atmosphere. _____

   **5.** Renewable resources produce more greenhouse gases than non-renewable resources. _____

4. Number the sentences to explain how acid rain forms and affects the environment. Write 1-5.

◯ Acid rain forms.

◯ Harmful gases are released into the atmosphere.

◯ Humans burn fossil fuels.

◯ Plants and animals are harmed and buildings made of some materials, like limestone, are damaged.

◯ Harmful gases react with water and oxygen in the atmosphere.

5. Match the actions with the effect they have on the environment. Write 1-6 in the boxes.

1. Water is wasted.

2. It increases the amount of carbon dioxide in the atmosphere.

3. Energy is conserved.

4. Living things in the sea are harmed.

5. Less waste is taken to landfill sites.

6. It reduces the amount of greenhouse gases that are released when food and garden waste decays in landfill sites.

A    B    C

D    E    F

# 6 Forces

## 6.1 What are mass and weight?

Keywords *balance   exert   force of gravity   hang
kilogram (kg)   mass   newton (N)   weight*

**Let's think**

When two objects have the same mass, they also weigh the same. But the mass and the weight of an object are not the same.

A

B

C

Mass is the amount of matter in an object. Mass can be measured in kilograms (kg) or grams (g) using a balance.

The Earth pulls all objects towards its centre by the force of gravity. Weight is the force of gravity pulling down on objects. Objects with bigger masses also have bigger weights. Since

weight is a force, its unit is the newton (N). We measure the weight of an object by hanging it from a force meter.

1. How much do the fruits in picture A weigh?

2. What is the mass of the fruit in picture B?

3. What is the weight of the keys in picture C?

## 👀 Let's explore!

- Investigate how 1 kg of mass has a weight of about 10 N on Earth.
- Measure the mass and the weight of different objects.
- Record your results.
- Discuss and draw a conclusion.

**(?)**  What is the pattern between mass and weight on Earth?

**B**

1. Any two objects that have mass are pulled together by the force of gravity. Moons, the Earth and other planets, and stars exert a force of gravity on other objects. The force of gravity depends on the mass of the objects. Objects with bigger masses exert a greater force of gravity on other objects. The Moon has a smaller mass than the Earth and therefore your weight on the Moon is about $\frac{1}{6}$ of your weight on Earth.

   On which planet would you weigh the most?

2. The force of gravity also depends on the distance between the objects. The further the objects are from each other, the weaker their force of gravity is.

   Is the force of gravity exerted on an astronaut less on the surface of the Earth or in an orbiting spacecraft?

 **What will your mass be on the Moon?**

 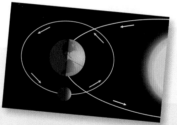

*Science in action*   Isaac Newton was a famous English scientist who explained that the same force that pulls us to the ground, the force of gravity, also keeps the Moon in orbit around the Earth. What force keeps the planets in orbit around the Sun?

- **Mass is the amount of matter in an object.**
- **Weight is the force of gravity pulling down on objects.**
- **Mass is measured in kilograms, while weight is measured in newtons.**
- **The weight of an object on Earth is about ten times its mass in kilograms.**
- **The force of gravity pulls any two objects that have mass together.**
- **The greater the mass of the objects and the closer they are to each other, the greater the force of gravity exerted on them.**

# 6.2 What are the effects of forces?

Keywords    compress   slow down   speed up

**Let's think**    We can't see forces. We can only see their effects.

! A force is a push or a pull.

A

A

B

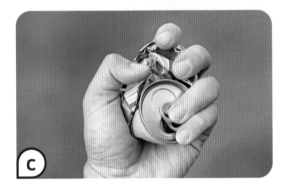
C

D

What do you think the effects of forces are?

## Let's explore!

- Investigate the effects of forces on objects.
- Do the test and record your observations.
- Discuss and draw a conclusion.

? What are the effects of forces?

A

**B**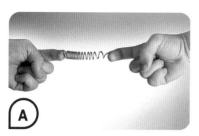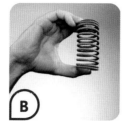

When an elastic material is stretched or compressed, it exerts an elastic force. An elastic force is exerted by a stretched or compressed spring trying to return to its normal length. Force meters have a spring inside. How do force meters work?

##  Let's explore!

- Investigate how a spring stretches if the force on it increases.
- Record your prediction.
- Do the test and record your results.
- Discuss and draw a conclusion.

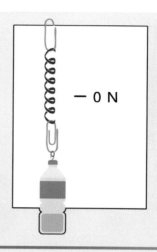

**?** How can we measure a force by the effect it has on the shape of an object?

**B**

*Science in action*

How does the force exerted by each player affect the ball?

- **Forces can make objects start and stop moving.**
- **Forces can make objects speed up or slow down.**
- **Forces can make objects change direction.**
- **Forces can change the shape of an object.**

# 6.3 How do forces act?

Keywords act   equal   force diagram   force pair

**Let's think**   All forces have both size and direction.

We draw force diagrams using arrows to show the forces acting on an object. The arrow shows the direction in which the force acts and its length shows the size of the force.

What does the arrow in the picture show?

## Let's explore!

- Investigate the direction in which forces in pairs act.
- Make predictions.
- Do the test and record your observations.
- Discuss and draw a conclusion.

A

- Compare the size that forces in pairs have.
- Make predictions.
- Do the test and record your results.
- Discuss and draw a conclusion.

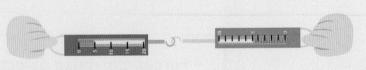

? How do forces act in pairs?

B

**B**

A

B

C

D

All forces act in pairs. If an object exerts a force on a second object, the second object exerts an equal and opposite force on the first. The forces in a force pair are exerted on different objects.

1. What forces are acting on the cars during the accident?

2. How do fish swim?

3. Why do swimmers push their feet against the wall?

4. What forces are acting between the Earth and the Moon?

*Science in action*

When a rocket burns fuel, hot gases come out of the back of the rocket and the rocket moves up. How do forces act in pairs to make the rocket move up into space?

- We draw force diagrams to show how forces act.
- Forces always act in pairs. The two forces are equal in size and act in opposite directions each on a different object.

# 6.4 How do forces affect movement?

**Keywords**   balanced   downwards   net force   speed   still
unbalanced   upwards

**Let's think**

Forces can change the speed and the direction in which an object is moving.

What forces are acting on the ball?

## 👀 Let's explore!

- Investigate the forces acting on a still object.
- Make predictions.
- Do the test and record your observations.
- Discuss and draw a conclusion.

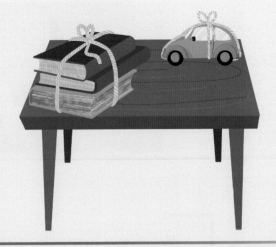

 How do forces act on a still object?

**B**

force of stalk

weight of apple

When an apple is hanging from a stalk its weight pulls it downwards and the force of the stalk pulls it upwards. These two forces have the same size but act in opposite directions. These are balanced forces and the net force acting on the apple is zero. Balanced forces don't change the movement of an object. This means that when an object is still because of the effect of balanced forces, it stays still, and when an object is moving under the effect of balanced forces its speed stays the same.

When the stalk breaks only the weight of the apple is acting on it. There is an unbalanced force acting on the apple and the net force is no longer zero. When two forces acting on an object have opposite directions but don't have the same size, they are unbalanced forces, and there is a net force acting on the object. Unbalanced forces cause changes in the movement of an object.

What will happen to the apple when the stalk breaks? Explain your answer.

 **Let's explore!**

- Investigate how the size of the force exerted on an object affects the distance the object will travel.
- Make predictions.
- Do the test and record your results.
- Discuss and draw a conclusion.

   How does the size of the force exerted on an object affect its movement?

**B**

*Science in action*

Why does the boat float on the water and what happens when it sinks?

- **An object stays still or moves at the same speed when the forces acting on it are balanced.**
- **An object changes movement when the forces acting on it are unbalanced.**

# 6.5 How does energy change?

Keywords  energy   kinetic energy   potential energy   ramp   transfer   work

**Let's think**

Objects need energy to move. Energy can change from one form into another, or it can be transferred from one object to another.

## A

Work is done when a force is acting on an object, causing the object to move. Whenever work is done, energy changes or energy is transferred. More work is done when the force acting on an object is bigger or the distance it moves is greater.

Is any work done in the pictures? Explain your answer.

## B

1. Objects can store energy that allows them to do work. This energy is called potential energy. There is potential energy in the food we eat, batteries and different kinds of fuel, an object that is at a height above the ground and an elastic object that has changed in shape. An object has more potential energy when it is higher above the ground than when it is on the ground. The greater the mass of an object at a height, the more potential energy it has. The more an elastic object has changed its shape, the more potential energy it has.
If the girls have the same mass, which girl has the most potential energy in picture A?

2. Every object that is moving has kinetic energy. The faster it moves and the greater its mass is, the more kinetic energy it has. If the yellow car is moving faster than the white car and their masses are the same, which car has the most kinetic energy in picture B?

## 👓 Let's explore!

- Investigate if the height of the ramp affects the distance the toy car travels.
- Make a prediction.
- Do the test and record your results.
- Repeat the measurements for different heights.
- Discuss and draw a conclusion.

 What changes of energy happen as the toy car travels down the ramp?

**A**

- Investigate if the length you compress the spring affects the distance the ball travels.
- Do the test and record your observations.
- Repeat the test by compressing the spring more.
- Discuss and draw a conclusion.

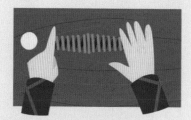

 What changes of energy happen when the spring is released?

**B**

*Science in action*

1. What change of energy is happening when the girl is moving down the slide?

2. Where does the boy get the energy from to play football?

- **Energy changes or energy is transferred when work is done.**
- **Objects that are at a height above the ground or elastic objects that have changed their shape have potential energy.**
- **Food, batteries and fuels also have potential energy.**
- **Moving objects have kinetic energy.**

# 6.6 What are the effects of friction?

**Keywords**   friction   grip   rub   slide   wear out

 **Let's think**

**Friction** is the force acting between two surfaces that are **sliding** or trying to slide across each other.

 When something vibrates, it makes a sound.

**A**

A

B

C

1. Why do tyres **wear out**?

2. How is sound made when we move the bow across the strings of the violin?

3. Why do we **rub** our hands when it is cold?

## 👀 Let's explore!

- Investigate the effects of friction.
- Do the test and record your observations.
- Discuss and draw a conclusion.

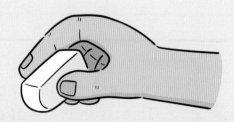

 What are the effects of friction?

**B**

push

friction

**A**

**B**

**C**

Friction acts in the opposite direction to the movement of the object. When you try to push an object across the floor friction makes it difficult. Friction makes objects grip on surfaces and not slip. Friction makes moving objects slow down and stop by changing their kinetic energy into heat.

Explain how friction can be useful and how friction can be a problem.

*Science in action*

The man is rubbing a wooden stick on a piece of wood to start a fire. How does this work?

- **Friction makes moving objects slow down and stop.**
- **Friction causes objects to wear out.**
- **Friction changes kinetic energy into heat.**
- **Friction produces sound.**

# 6.7 What factors affect friction?

**Keywords**  *surface area*

**Let's think**  Friction is different between different objects and surfaces.

What do you think the factors that affect friction between two surfaces are?

 If there is more friction you will need more force to move an object.

## Let's explore!

- Investigate if the types of the surfaces sliding across each other affect the amount of friction produced.
- Make predictions.
- Plan a fair test.
- Do the test and record your results.
- Repeat the measurements.
- Discuss and draw a conclusion.

**A**

- Investigate if the weight of the object sliding across a surface affects the amount of friction produced.
- Make predictions.
- Plan a fair test.
- Do the test and record your results.
- Discuss and draw a conclusion.

**B**

##  Let's explore!

- Investigate if the surface area of the object sliding across a surface affects the amount of friction produced.
- Make predictions.
- Do the test and record your results.
- Discuss and draw a conclusion.

**(?)** What are the factors that affect friction? What doesn't affect friction?

**C**

*Science in action*

When is the lorry more likely to slip on a wet road: when it is filled with pieces of wood or when it is empty?

- **The rougher the surfaces that are sliding across each other, the greater the friction acting between them.**
- **The greater the weight of the object, the more friction is acting on it.**
- **The surface area of the object sliding across a surface is not a factor that affects friction.**

# 6.8 How can we reduce and increase friction?

Keywords  *lubricant   roller*

**Let's think**

Friction is an important force. Without friction we would not be able to walk, but friction always slows down moving objects. Sometimes we want friction to be great and sometimes we want it to be small.

1. Why is the man using a hand pallet truck to move the boxes?
2. Why do we put lubricant on the bicycle chain?
3. Why do we wear shoes with rough soles when we go trekking?

## 👀 Let's explore!

- Investigate how rollers affect friction.
- Make predictions.
- Do the test and record your results.
- Discuss and draw a conclusion.

**A**

- Investigate how lubricants affect friction.
- Make predictions.
- Do the test and record your results.
- Discuss and draw a conclusion.

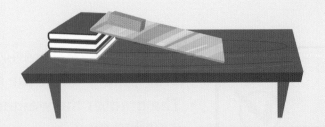

(?) How can we reduce friction?

**B**

# How can we increase friction?

**B**

A

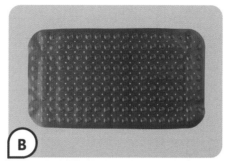

B

C

D

Sometimes it is useful to increase friction and sometimes it is useful to reduce friction.

Give examples of where it is useful to increase friction and examples of where it is useful to reduce friction.

*Science in action*

Why do we have to drive carefully on a wet road?

- **Rollers and lubricants reduce friction between two surfaces.**
- **We can increase friction by making the surfaces that slide across each other rougher or by increasing the weight of the object sliding across a surface.**

# 6.9 What is air resistance?

**Keywords**  *air resistance*  *drop*  *parachute*  *streamlined*

 **Let's think**   Liquids and gases also exert a force on objects that move through them.

Aristotle (384-322 BCE) believed that heavy objects would always fall to the ground before light objects. The heavier an object, the quicker it would fall. Aristotle never tested this to find out. Galileo Galilei (1564-1642) tested Aristotle's theory by dropping two balls of the same size but different mass from the Tower of Pisa.

What do you think Galileo found out?

## Let's explore!

- Investigate if a heavier object falls faster than a lighter object.
- Make a prediction.
- Make it a fair test.
- Do the test and record your observations.
- Discuss and draw a conclusion.

 What force affects the time it takes for an object that falls through air to fall to the ground?

A

**B**

A

B

When an object moves through air, a force of air resistance is acting in the opposite direction to movement. The particles of different gases in the air hit the object and slow it down.

What factors affect air resistance?

 **Let's explore!**

- Investigate how the size of a parachute affects the time it takes to land.
- Make predictions.
- Do the test and record your results.
- Repeat your measurements.
- Discuss and draw a conclusion.

**?** How does the surface area of an object affect the air resistance acting on it?

**B**

 What other variables could you test to find out if they affect the air resistance acting on a parachute?

*Science in action*

1. How does a parachute help a space shuttle stop when it lands?

2. Why do high-speed trains have a streamlined shape?

- **Air resistance is a force acting on objects that move through air.**
- **Air resistance slows down objects.**
- **The greater the surface area and the speed of a moving object, the more air resistance acts on it.**

# 6 ⚛ Review

Go to the **Unit maps** section at the back of the book.

1. **Complete the sentences with the words/phrase in the box.**

   balance   force   force meter   kilograms   mass   matter   newtons   weight

   **1.** Weight is the _____ of gravity pulling on objects. Mass is the amount of _____ in an object.

   **2.** Mass is measured in _____ using a _____.
   Weight is measured in _____ using a _____.

   **3.** Our _____ will stay the same but our _____ will change if we go to the Moon.

2. **Look at the picture. Draw arrows (→) to show the forces acting on the boat. Then answer the question.**

   Are the forces balanced or unbalanced? Explain your answer.

3. **Read the sentences. Write Yes or No.**

   **1.** Forces always act in pairs. _____

   **2.** More friction is acting on an object that is sliding on its big surface than on its small surface. _____

   **3.** Less friction is acting on a lorry full of wood than when it is empty. _____

   **4.** An object begins to move when the forces acting on it are unbalanced. _____

   **5.** Friction causes objects to wear out. _____

   **6.** Lubricants increase friction between two surfaces. _____

4. Look at the picture of a wooden block sliding down a plastic ramp. Then answer the questions.

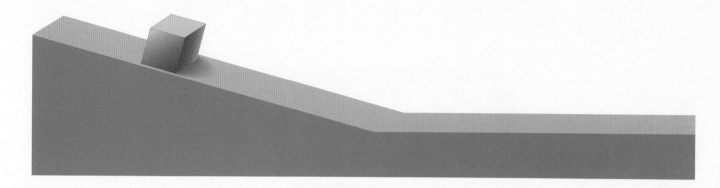

1. What form of energy does the block have at the top of the ramp?

2. What change of energy is happening while the block is travelling down the ramp?

3. What force makes the block finally stop?

4. How will the distance the block travels change if the height of the ramp increases? Explain your answer.

5. How will the distance the block travels change if it moves on carpet rather than on plastic? Explain your answer.

5. Write the names of the forces acting on the parachute in boxes A and B. Then answer the question.

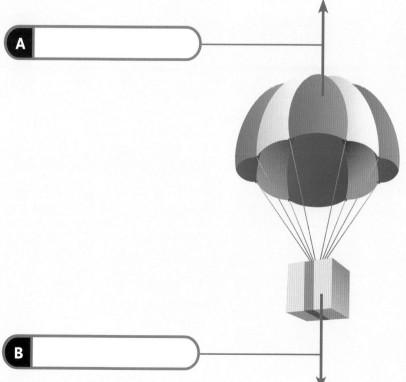

A

B

How will the time the parachute takes to fall to the ground change if we increase the size of the parachute? Explain your answer.

# 1 Body Systems

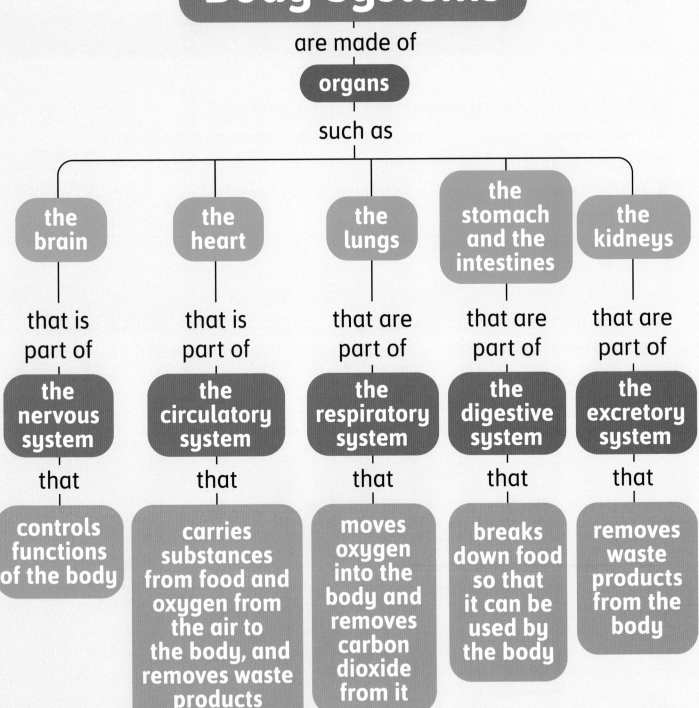

**Body Systems**

are made of

organs

such as

| the brain | the heart | the lungs | the stomach and the intestines | the kidneys |
|---|---|---|---|---|
| that is part of | that is part of | that are part of | that are part of | that are part of |
| the nervous system | the circulatory system | the respiratory system | the digestive system | the excretory system |
| that | that | that | that | that |
| controls functions of the body | carries substances from food and oxygen from the air to the body, and removes waste products away from it | moves oxygen into the body and removes carbon dioxide from it | breaks down food so that it can be used by the body | removes waste products from the body |

# 2 Reversible and Irreversible Changes in Materials

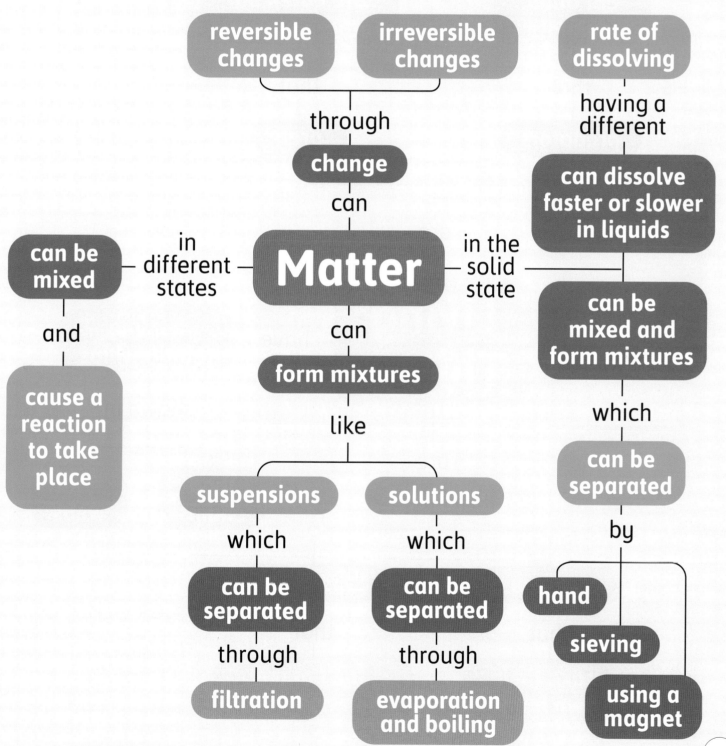

reversible changes

irreversible changes

rate of dissolving

through

having a different

change

can

can dissolve faster or slower in liquids

can be mixed

in different states

**Matter**

in the solid state

and

can

can be mixed and form mixtures

cause a reaction to take place

form mixtures

which

like

can be separated

suspensions

solutions

by

which

which

hand

can be separated

can be separated

sieving

through

through

using a magnet

filtration

evaporation and boiling

# 3 Feeding Relationships

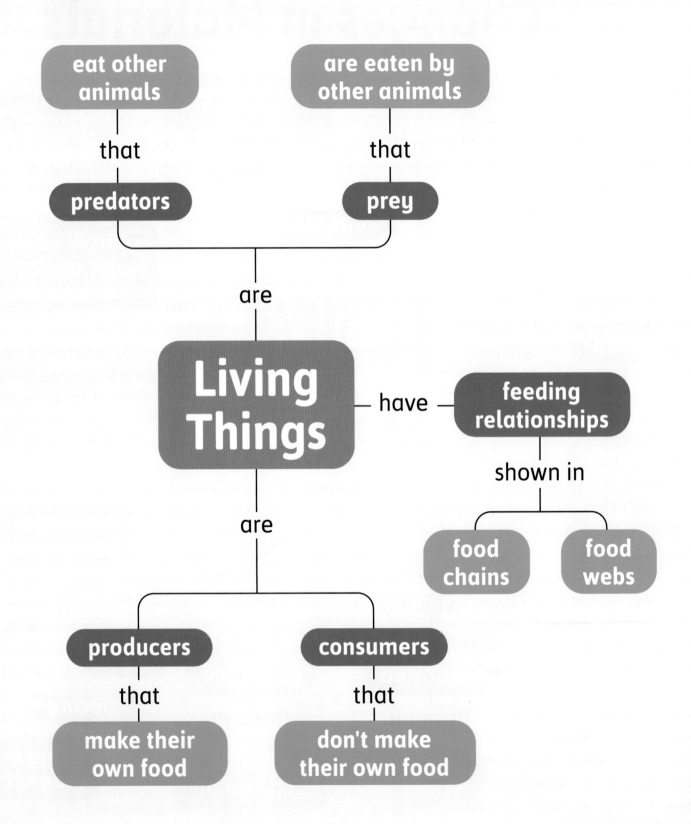

eat other animals

that

predators

are eaten by other animals

that

prey

are

**Living Things**

have

feeding relationships

shown in

food chains

food webs

are

producers

that

make their own food

consumers

that

don't make their own food

# 4  Electricity

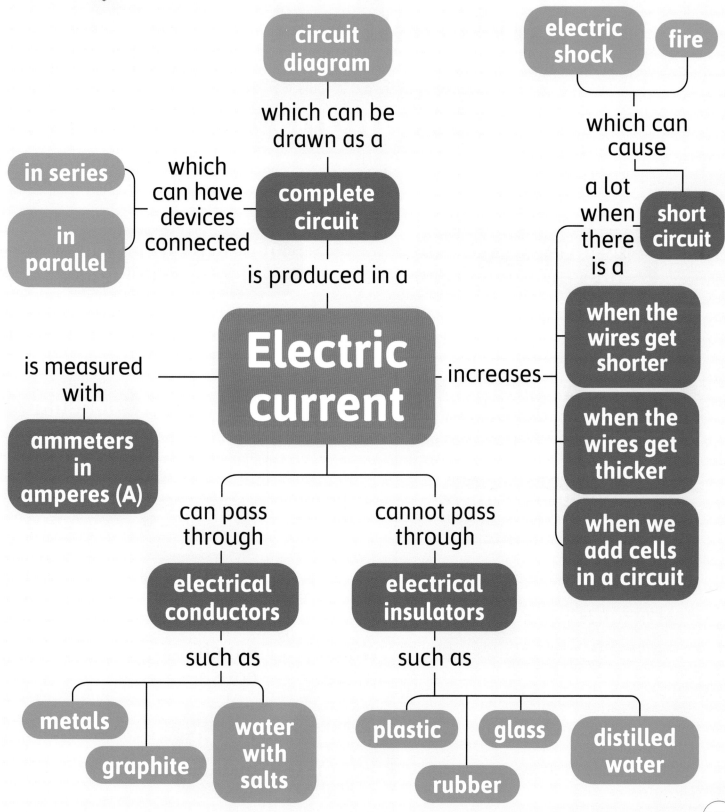

circuit diagram

which can be drawn as a

complete circuit

which can have devices connected

in series

in parallel

is produced in a

# Electric current

is measured with

ammeters in amperes (A)

can pass through

electrical conductors

such as

metals

graphite

water with salts

cannot pass through

electrical insulators

such as

plastic

glass

rubber

distilled water

increases

when the wires get shorter

when the wires get thicker

when we add cells in a circuit

electric shock

fire

which can cause

a lot when there is a

short circuit

# 5  Humans and the Environment

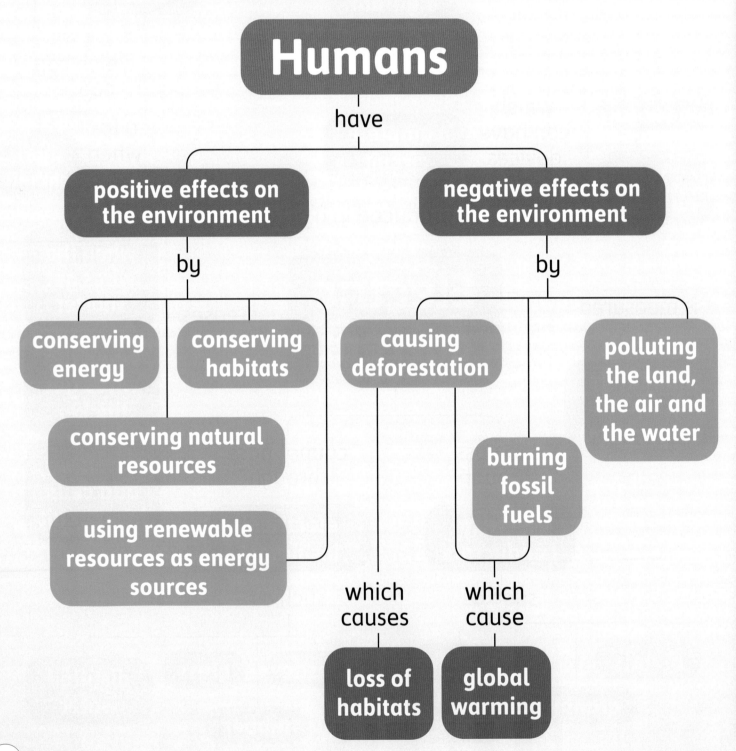

# 6  Forces

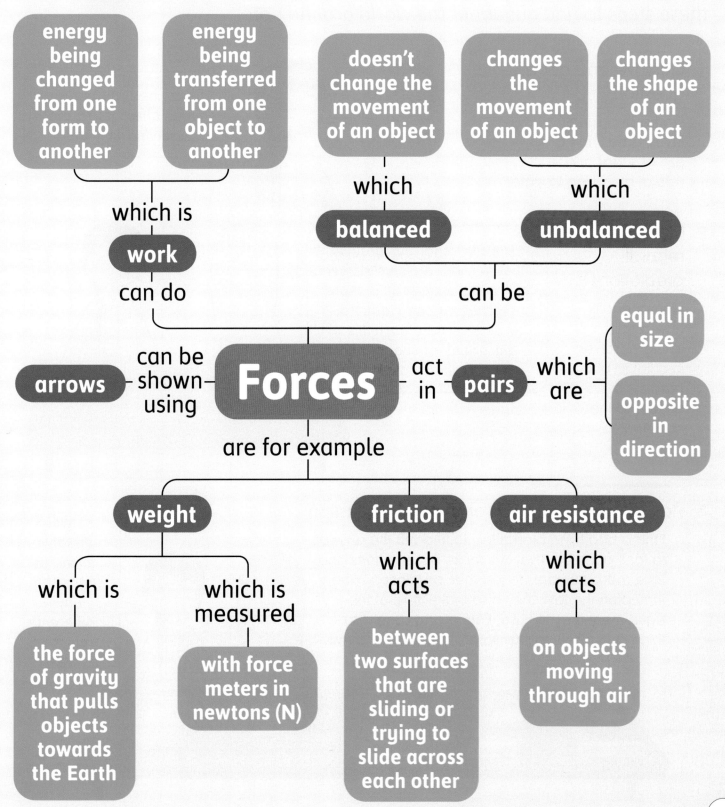

energy being changed from one form to another

energy being transferred from one object to another

which is

**work**

can do

doesn't change the movement of an object

which

**balanced**

changes the movement of an object

changes the shape of an object

which

**unbalanced**

can be

**arrows**

can be shown using

**Forces**

act in

**pairs**

which are

equal in size

opposite in direction

are for example

**weight**

which is

the force of gravity that pulls objects towards the Earth

which is measured

with force meters in newtons (N)

**friction**

which acts

between two surfaces that are sliding or trying to slide across each other

**air resistance**

which acts

on objects moving through air

# Work like a scientist

## Steps of the scientific method

*Scientists study different things, like animals, plants, materials and phenomena. They follow some steps to do this. You can follow some of these steps to find out about the world around you.*

### 1. Observe and ask a question

Emma and Luna investigate if the grain size of sugar affects its rate of dissolving in water.

Does the grain size of sugar affect its rate of dissolving in water?

### 2. Make and record predictions

Emma recalls how a solid solute dissolves in a liquid and predicts the answer to the question.

I predict that big grains of sugar will dissolve slower in water, because it is more difficult for the water to go between the particles of big grains of sugar than smaller grains.

### 3. Plan an investigation to answer your question

a. Emma and Luna plan a test to find out the answer to their question. They will make observations and take measurements to test their prediction. When they plan the test, they also make a list of the equipment they will use. Emma and Luna also think about how to stay safe while doing the test.

I will dissolve forms of sugar that have different grain sizes in water.

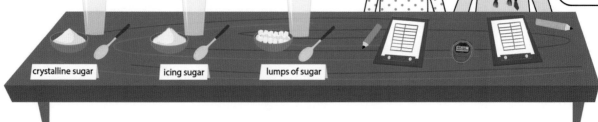

crystalline sugar    icing sugar    lumps of sugar

b. Emma and Luna think about how to make the test fair. They identify the variables that may affect the investigation. They will change one variable and see if and how it affects another.

I will only change the grain size of the sugar.

I will keep the stirring and the temperature of the water the same. I will also use the same amount of sugar and water each time.

I will measure the time needed for each form of sugar to dissolve in the water.

crystalline sugar    icing sugar    lumps of sugar

## 4. Do the test and record your results

Emma and Luna put a different form of sugar in each cup, stir the solutions, and measure the time needed for the sugar to dissolve in each cup. They repeat the investigation one more time, and then they find the mean time needed for each form of sugar to dissolve in each cup.

crystalline sugar    icing sugar    lumps of sugar

## 5. Discuss and draw a conclusion

Emma and Luna look at their results and compare them to their prediction. Then they draw a conclusion and share it with the class.

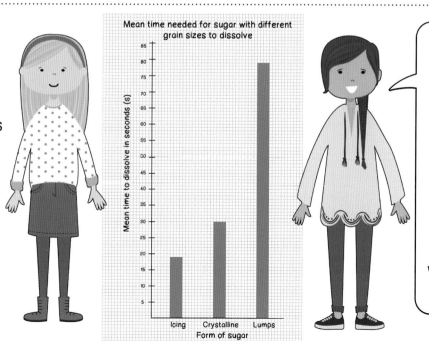

Mean time needed for sugar with different grain sizes to dissolve

Mean time to dissolve in seconds (s)

Icing    Crystalline    Lumps
Form of sugar

The grain size of sugar is a factor that affects its rate of dissolving in water. The bigger the grain size of the solid, the slower it will dissolve in the solvent.

# Searching for information

## 1. Using books and encyclopedias

When we want to search for information about something, we can use books and encyclopedias. First, we should think about some words that describe the information we want to search for, called keywords. Then, we have to look at the title of the book, the text on the back cover, the contents pages and the index at the back of the book to find these keywords. Then, we have to search for these keywords inside the book.

title

text

back cover

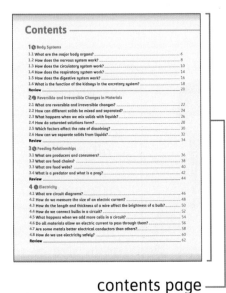

contents page

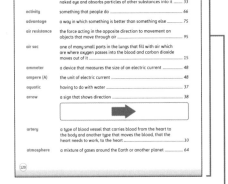

Index

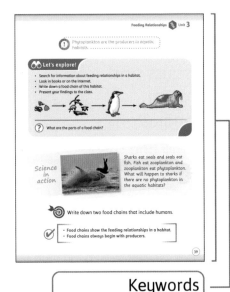

Keywords
food chain,
feeding relationships,
habitat, producer

## 2. Using the Internet

When we want to search for information about something, we can also use the Internet.

Students can use search engines designed for children, like Kid's Search, Kiddle, etc. To use them, you have to type some keywords in the search engine, and look at the results. Website addresses or URLs that end with .edu or .gov usually have reliable information. To find out if a website is reliable, you have to look for the name of the author and when the article was written. Also, you have to look if the author's job is written in the article, and if the article is written in a scientific book, scientific magazine, etc. Websites that have a lot of advertisements are often not reliable. You should also try to find the same information in more than one website to be sure it is reliable.

You have to choose websites that have information written in a simple enough way for you to understand. Online encyclopedias, and websites designed for children, have reliable information written in a simple way.

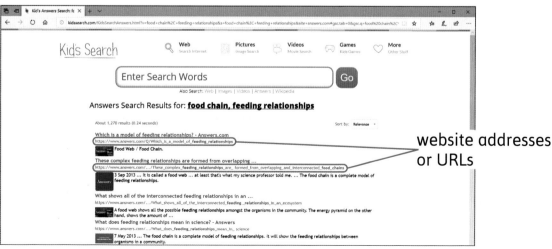

website addresses or URLs

107

# Using patterns

1. In the results of an investigation there is often a pattern. We can use this pattern to draw conclusions.

   a. Dennis and Enzo do a test to find out how the brightness of a bulb changes as they add more cells in a simple circuit.

   b. Dennis and Enzo record their results in a table.

   | Number of cells in the simple circuit | Brightness of bulb |
   |---|---|
   | 1 | normal |
   | 2 | bright |
   | 3 | very bright |

   c. Dennis and Enzo look at the pattern in their results and draw a conclusion.

   Enzo, there is a pattern in our results. Do you recognise it?

   Yes, I recognise it. So, the conclusion we can draw is that as we add more cells in a simple circuit, the bulb shines more brightly.

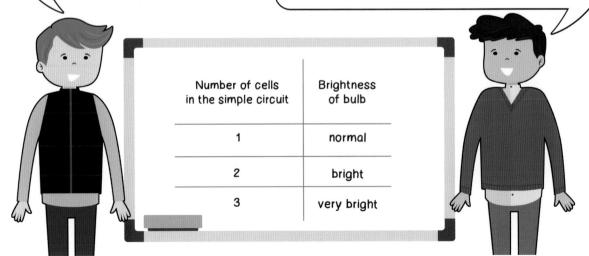

| Number of cells in the simple circuit | Brightness of bulb |
|---|---|
| 1 | normal |
| 2 | bright |
| 3 | very bright |

## 2. We can also use patterns to see if our results are reliable.

a. Maya and Yin do a test to find out how the size of a parachute affects the time it takes to land.

b. Maya and Yin record their results in a table.

| Size of parachute in square centimetres (cm²) | First measurement: time to land in seconds (s) | Second measurement: time to land in seconds (s) | Third measurement: time to land in seconds (s) |
|---|---|---|---|
| 400 | 2.05 | 2.20 | 1.99 |
| 900 | 2.17 | 2.21 | 2.15 |
| 1600 | 2.35 | 2.39 | 2.00 |

c. Maya and Yin suppose that the measurements for each parachute size will be almost the same. But they see two measurements that are very different from the others.

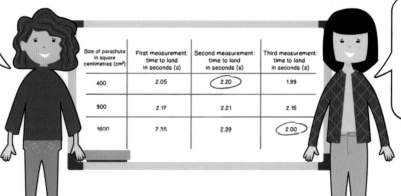

Yin there are two measurements that do not follow the pattern that the time to land increases as the size of the parachute increases. What should we do?

Let's repeat our investigation, and take two new measurements.

d. Maya and Yin repeat their investigation and take two new measurements. They found out that the measurements they took the first time were not correct.

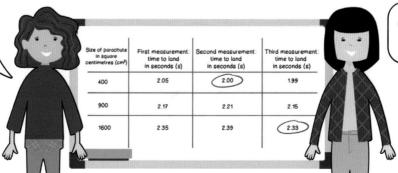

The two new measurements we took follow the pattern. The measurements we took the first time were not correct.

Our results are reliable now.

# Presenting results in a line graph

1. Sono has recorded his results in a table about how the time needed for sugar to dissolve changes as the temperature of the water changes.

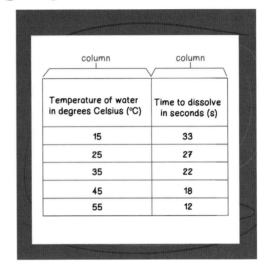

| column | column |
|---|---|
| Temperature of water in degrees Celsius (ºC) | Time to dissolve in seconds (s) |
| 15 | 33 |
| 25 | 27 |
| 35 | 22 |
| 45 | 18 |
| 55 | 12 |

2. Sono will present his results in a line graph. A line graph is a drawing in which we connect points with straight lines. We use line graphs to show how one variable is affected when another variable is changed. On the horizontal axis, we put the variable we change, and on the vertical axis the variable we measure. To make a line graph, Sono will use graph paper.

   a. Sono writes a heading for the line graph.

   b. Sono puts the temperature of the water on the horizontal axis and the time needed for the sugar to dissolve on the vertical axis. Each point on the drawing will show the time needed for sugar to dissolve in water at a different temperature.

   c. Sono draws the points for all his results on the graph paper. Then he connects one point to the next by drawing a straight line between them. This is the line graph he made.

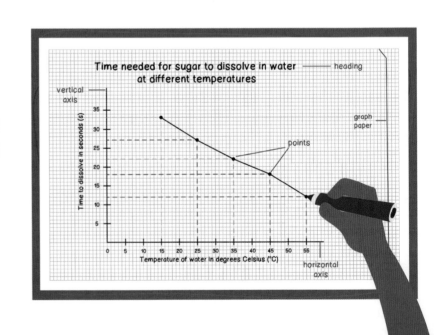

# Using a force meter

1. We use force meters to measure forces. The most common unit of force is the newton (N). Some force meters also have a scale for measuring mass in grams. If you have this kind of force meter, you can use this to measure mass, and not a balance.

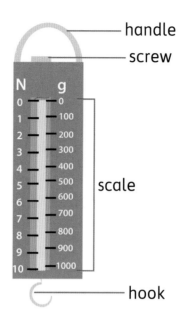

2. Hold the handle of the force meter with one hand. The force meter should show zero on the scale. If not, turn the screw to set the force meter to zero.

3. Attach the force meter to the object, and pull the object at the same speed slowly until the object begins to slide across the surface. Move the force meter parallel to the surface. Read the force meter while the object is moving.

4. Hang the object from the force meter and read the scale at eye level.

# Materials

A3 white card

bread

coloured markers

glue

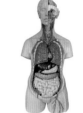

human torso model

iodine solution

paper towel

plastic cup

plate

scissors

stopwatch

string

water

## Unit 2 Reversible and Irreversible Changes in Materials

aluminium foil

beaker

beans

bicarbonate of soda

bottle

bowl

candle with holder

conical flask

filter paper

flour

funnel

gloves

lentils

magnet

paper clip

pepper

plaster of Paris

plastic cup

plate

salt

sand

scales

sieve

spoon

sticky notes

stirring rod

stopwatch

sugar

thermometer

vinegar

volumetric
cylinder

washer

water

## Unit 3 Feeding Relationships

A4 white card

aluminium foil

beaker

bread

coloured
markers

forceps

hotplate

iodine solution

magnifying
glass

paper towel

plant

plate

potato

surgical spirit

water

# Unit 4 Electricity

 aluminium foil

 ammeter

 batteries

 bulb

 bulb holder

 buzzer

 cardboard

 cell

 compass

 copper wire

 crocodile clip

 distilled water

 glass

 insulating tape

 magnet

 motor

 nail

 nichrome wire

 paper clip

 paper fastener

 pencil

 rubber bands

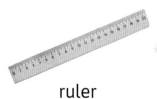 ruler

salt

 spoon

steel wire

steel wool

sticky tape

straw

toothpicks

wire

wooden stick

# Unit 5 Humans and the Environment

A3 white card

aluminium can

aluminium foil

bicarbonate of soda

Blu-Tack

bottle

chalk

cling film

coloured markers

jar

milk carton

newspaper

plastic cup

rubber bands

scissors

shampoo bottle

sticky notes

sticky tape

straw

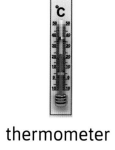
thermometer

vinegar

water

wrapping paper

# Unit 6 Forces

A3 card

A4 paper

aluminium foil

bag of beans

balloon

beaker

block

book

bottle

cardboard

coloured markers

dustbin bag

force meter

magnet

oil

paper clip

paper towel

pencil case

plastic bag

plastic cup

rubber

rubber bands

ruler

sandpaper

scales

scissors

screw ring

set square

soft rubber ball

soft tape measure

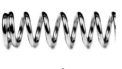

spring

sticky tape

stone

stopwatch

string

table tennis ball

teaspoon

tennis ball

toy car

washer

water

waxed paper

# Glossary

**balance**  a device that measures mass ................................................................ 78

**balanced**  when two forces have the same size but act on an object in opposite directions .................................................................................. 85

**be poor in**  used to describe that something has very little of another thing .... 11

**be rich in**  used to describe that something has a lot of another thing ........... 11

**beat**  to make the same movement and sound again and again .............. 12

**blood**  a red liquid inside the body that carries oxygen, substances from food and waste products .............................................................. 10

**blood vessel**  a part of the circulatory system that blood passes through ........... 10

**body system**  a set of organs in the body that have a specific function ............... 6

*The body systems in our body work together to give our body everything it needs.*

**bow***  a long, thin piece of wood with horse hair stretched from one end to the other which people use to play musical instruments, like the violin ............................................................................................. 88

**brain**  the organ in the head that helps many important functions of the body to happen ..................................................................................... 6

Parts of the brain

cerebrum

cerebellum

brainstem 8

**encyclopedia***  a book or a set of books which give information about one or many different things, usually arranged in the same order as the letters A, B, C, D, etc.; a similar group of articles on the Internet ............................................................. 106

**endangered**  being a species that might not exist soon ................................. 65

**energy**  the ability to do work or to cause a change ........................... 86

*A lot of energy is needed to move the heavy box across the room.*

**energy source**  something that produces energy ........................................... 48

**enhanced**  being increased ...................................................................... 64

**equal**  being the same in size, number, etc. as something else .................... 83

**excretion**  the process of removing waste products from the body ................. 18

**excretory system**  the system that removes waste products from the body .............. 18

**exert**  to use a force on an object ...................................................... 79

**explore**  to examine something carefully ................................................ 43

**extinct**  being a species that does not exist any more .............................. 65

**factor**  a thing among others that affects something ............................... 30

**feeding relationship**  the way in which living things are connected in a habitat because of what eats or is eaten by what ................................. 38

**filament**  a thin wire inside a light bulb ............................................... 59

**filter (noun)**  an object with tiny holes that works like a sieve, and collects only the materials that cannot fit through its holes ....................... 33

**filter (verb)**  to remove substances from a liquid or a gas that are not wanted ......................................................................... 18

**filtration**  a process through which we can separate a liquid from an insoluble solid using filters ..................................................... 32

**flame***

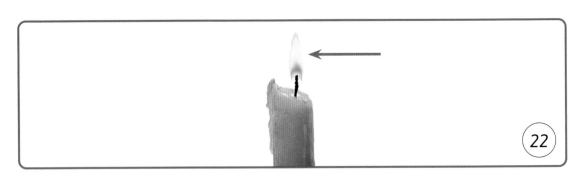

(22)

92

**length** — the measure of how long something is ........................ 50

**level\*** — the amount of something ........................ 64

**liver** — the organ that produces a digestive juice, stores substances from food, and removes harmful substances from the blood ........ 17

**loss** — the fact of a habitat not existing any more ........................ 65

**lubricant** — a substance you put on a surface or inside an engine so that friction is reduced ........................ 92

**lump (of soil)\*** — a solid piece of something that is a bit bigger than other pieces usually are ........................ 25

**lump (of sugar)\*** — a piece of sugar having the shape of a cube with each side having 1 cm length ........................ 30

**lung** — one of the two organs that humans and many animals use for breathing ........................ 6

**major** — important ........................ 6

**marine\*** — having to do with the sea and the living things there ........................ 71

**mass** — the amount of matter in an object ........................ 78

**medicine tablet\*** — a form of medicine in the solid state that is small, round and flat ........................ 27

**message** — information that is carried to and from the brain ........................ 9

**microplastics** — small pieces of plastic, less than 5 mm long, that can be harmful to species that live in the sea, like fish ........................ 68

**mine\***     holes people make in the ground to remove materials, like coal and metals ....... 73

**mix**     to put different materials together so they become one ............... 24

**mixture**     a combination of materials or substances that are put together, but are not joined with each other ............... 24

*Air is a mixture of gases like oxygen, carbon dioxide, water vapour, etc.*

**multimeter\***     a device that can measure both electric current and voltage ....... 48

**narrow\***     not being wide ............... 13

**natural gas**     a kind of gas we find below the surface of the Earth, that is used as a fuel ............... 73

**needle\***     a long, thin piece of metal ............... 49

**negative**     being harmful or bad ............... 70

**nerve**     a part of the nervous system that carries messages between the brain and other parts of the body ............... 8

**nervous system**     the system that controls functions of the body, like movement ... 8

**net force**     the sum of all the forces acting on an object ............... 85

**newton (N)**     a unit of force ............... 78

**nitrogen\***     a gas that makes up most of the air ............... 14

**non-renewable (resources)**     when something cannot be replaced by nature in a short time ............... 74

*Coal is a non-renewable resource, because it needs millions of years to form.*

**oesophagus**     a part of the digestive system through which food passes from the mouth to the stomach ............... 16

**organ**     a part of the body that has a specific function ............... 6

*The brain is a very important organ we cannot live without.*

**parachute**    a large piece of fabric that is attached to people or objects that fall from a plane and opens in the air to make them fall slowly to the ground ........................................................................ 95

**parallel***    when the distance between two or more objects, paths, lines, etc. is the same all along their length ............................................. 111

**parallel circuit**    a circuit that has more than one path for the electric current to pass through ......................................................... 52

**patch***    a small area of something, that is different from the area around it ................................................................................................. 69

**phenomenon*** **(pl. phenomena)**    something that is observed to be happening or existing .............. 104

**photosynthesis**    the process through which plants make their own food ................... 36

**physical change**    a change in the shape, state or appearance of a material ............. 22

**phytoplankton**    very small living things that live in water and produce their own food through photosynthesis .................................................. 37

**pipeline***    a long tube, usually under the ground, that carries gases or liquids over long distances ................................................................. 74

**platform***    a surface over the sea on which equipment stands and people work to get crude oil and natural gas ...................................... 73

| | |
|---|---|
| **recycling** | the action of collecting things that have been used, and changing them to make something new that can be used again ... 68 |
| **release*** | to stop holding something ........................................................ 87 |
| **remove** | to take something away from a thing or place ...................... 10 |
| **renewable (resources)** | being replaced by nature ............................................................ 74 |
| | *Wind is a renewable resource, because there is no end to the amount of wind that is formed on the Earth.* |
| **repeat** | to do something again or more than once .............................. 50 |
| **replace*** | to make new things when those things were used and finished ... 74 |
| **resource** | something that exists in nature and people can use, like coal, wind, water, etc. ................................................................... 72 |
| **respiration** | the process of releasing energy from food ........................... 15 |
| **respiratory system** | the system that moves oxygen around the body and removes carbon dioxide from it ................................................. 14 |
| **reversible** | that can be changed and brought back to the original state ......... 22 |
| | *Freezing water into ice is a reversible change, you heat it up and it melts back into water.* |
| **rocket*** | a spacecraft with a cylindrical shape .................................... 83 |

| | |
|---|---|
| **roller** | a cylindrical wheel that turns to carry something .................. 92 |

| | | |
|---|---|---|
| **rub** | to move one object against another ................................................... | 88 |
| **rust (noun)** | a substance with a red-brown colour that forms on iron or steel objects, when they come into contact with oxygen from the air or water ............................................................................. | 23 |

| | | |
|---|---|---|
| **rust (verb)** | to be covered with a red-brown substance, as a result of coming into contact with oxygen from the air or water ................. | 23 |

*After we returned from the trip we saw that the bicycle had rusted because it had stayed outside the house the whole summer.*

| | | |
|---|---|---|
| **saliva** | the liquid that is produced in the mouth ................................. | 16 |
| **salt\*** | a substance, like sea salt ......................................................... | 18, 57 |
| **saturated** | being a solution that has had the largest possible amount of a solute dissolved into it until no more can dissolve ................. | 29 |
| **scientific\*** | having to do with science ....................................................... | 104, 107 |
| **search engine\*** | a computer program used for searching for information on the Internet ..................................................................... | 107 |
| **separate** | to cause something not to be a part of something else; to cause something to be apart from something else ........................ | 24 |
| **series circuit** | a circuit that has only one path for the electric current to pass through ..................................................................... | 52 |
| **shellfish\*** | kinds of animals with a shell that live in water .................. | 68 |

| | |
|---|---|
| **short circuit** | a bad connection in a circuit that causes the electric current to pass through a shorter path ................................................... 60 |
| **sieve (noun)** | an object that has holes, and collects only the pieces of those materials that are not small enough to pass through the holes ... 25 |

| | |
|---|---|
| **sieve (verb)** | to separate solid materials of different sizes by putting them through a sieve ............................................................... 25 |
| **simple\*** | being made of only a few parts ......................................... 16 |
| **sink\*** | to go below the surface of a liquid ................................... 85 |
| **slide** | to move across a surface ................................................. 88 |
| **slow down** | to move more slowly ....................................................... 81 |
| **small intestine** | a part of the digestive system that food goes into after passing through the stomach ..................................................... 16 |
| **solar panel** | a piece of equipment that absorbs light from the Sun, and is used to produce electrical energy and for heating ................. 74 |
| **sole\*** | the surface under the shoe ........................................ 60, 92 |
| **soluble** | that can dissolve in a liquid, forming a solution .................. 27 |
| **solute** | the solid substance that dissolves into another liquid substance ...................................................................... 28 |
| **solution** | a type of mixture that forms after a soluble solid dissolves in a liquid and the mixture has a transparent appearance .......... 27 |
| **solvent** | a liquid that another substance dissolves into .................... 28 |
| **space shuttle\*** | a spacecraft that travels into space and back to the Earth ........... 95 |
| **species** | a group of animals, plants, etc. with similar characteristics that can reproduce with each other, and create new animals, plants, etc. that are also able to reproduce ............................... 36 |

| | | |
|---|---|---|
| **specific*** | connected with only one thing; being an amount that does not change, and can only be that amount | 6, 29 |
| **speech*** | the ability to speak | 8 |
| | *After the accident he lost his speech.* | |
| **speed** | the rate at which somebody or something moves | 84 |
| **speed up** | to move faster | 81 |
| **spinal cord** | the nerves inside the spine that connect the brain to the body | 8 |
| **spring*** | | 81 |

| | | |
|---|---|---|
| **stalk*** | a thin part of a plant that holds a leaf, a flower or a fruit | 85 |
| **starch** | a kind of carbohydrate that is made up of glucose and gives us energy | 36 |
| **still** | not moving | 84 |
| **stir** | to move an object, like a spoon, inside a liquid material to mix it in a better way | 30 |
| **stomach** | the organ where food is turned into a liquid mixture | 6 |
| **streamlined** | when something has a shape that causes less air resistance to act on it | 95 |
| **suggest** | to propose a plan, an idea, etc. | 71 |
| **surface area** | the size of the outside part of something | 91 |
| **suspension** | a type of mixture that forms after an insoluble solid is added to a liquid and the mixture has a translucent appearance | 27 |
| **symbol** | a shape, or an image we use to show something | 46 |
| **thick** | not being thin | 50 |
| **thickness** | the distance between two opposite surfaces of something | 50 |

**thought***  an idea, a picture, etc. you have in your brain ............................ 8

**trachea**  a part of the respiratory system that carries air to and from the lungs ............................................................................ 14

**transfer**  to move from one place or object to another ....................... 86

**treat***  to try to make a person that has an illness healthy again ............. 17

**trend**  a general direction of how results change ........................... 12

*In the past few years, there has been a trend for families to have fewer children.*

**tungsten***  a metal that has the highest melting point and is used to make filaments in light bulbs ......................................... 59

**tunnel***  a passage that people build under the ground ...................... 73

**unbalanced**  when only one force acts on an object or when two forces act on an object in opposite directions but don't have the same size ......................................................................... 85

**upwards**  moving or showing towards a higher place ......................... 85

**urea**  a substance that the kidneys remove from the body ............. 18

**urine**  a liquid excreted from the body that is made of water with waste products dissolved in it ........................................ 18

**vein**  a type of blood vessel that carries blood from the body to the heart ............................................................................ 10

**volt (V)**  the unit of voltage ......................................................... 54

**voltage**  a measure of the electrical energy given to the flowing particles in a circuit ....................................................................... 54

**washing powder*** a solid substance used as soap in washing machines to clean clothes ........ 31

**wear out** to become damaged because something is used a lot .......... 88

**weight** the force of gravity pulling down on objects .......... 78

**wheelchair***

9

**wind turbine** a tall structure that has large blades that are turned around by the wind, and is used to produce electrical energy .......... 74

**work** the amount of energy transferred from one object to another or changed from one form to another .......... 86

**write down** to record something on a piece of paper .......... 39

**zooplankton** very small kinds of animals that live in water and eat other living things .......... 37

# Notes

**Notes**

**Notes**

**International Primary**
**SCIENCE 6**
**Student's Book**

First published by:   **Vector M & S Publishing**

www.vectormsint.com

Offices, associated companies and representatives throughout the world

Copyright © 2021 Vector M & S Publishing

We would like to thank Shutterstock, 123RF and NASA for permission to reproduce copyright photographs.

The publishers have tried to contact all copyright holders, but in cases where they may have failed, they will be pleased to make the necessary arrangements at the first opportunity.

Produced in the EU

ISBN: 978-618-5305-67-3                                                              N2006002542-1717